"[MARK TWAIN] WAS THE FIRST AMERICAN
OF WORLD RANK TO WRITE IN A GENUINELY
COLLOQUIAL AND NATIVE AMERICAN."
—H. L. Mencken

**Mark Twain once said: "A classic is something
that everybody wants to have read but nobody
wants to read." But this collection shows that—
for once!—Twain was wrong. These classic gems
are so entertaining that once you begin reading,
you won't want to put them down. You'll discover
an entire anthology of hilarious selections like:**

Mark Twain once attended a dinner party at
which the subject of heaven and hell was raised.
Throughout the heated discussion Twain said
nothing. Finally, the hostess asked, "Why
haven't you said something, Mr. Clemens?
Surely you must have an opinion on the
subject."

"Madame, you must excuse me," Mark Twain
replied. "I am silent because of necessity. I have
friends in both places."

. . . and much, much more from America's favorite
humorist—

THE WIT & WISDOM OF MARK TWAIN

ALEX AYRES is senior editor and part owner of *Running
Times,* and his epigrams have appeared in *Forbes.* While in
college, Mr. Ayres was editor of the *Harvard Lampoon,* the
nation's oldest humor magazine.

THE
WIT & WISDOM
OF
MARK TWAIN

edited by Alex Ayres

A MERIDIAN BOOK

MERIDIAN
Published by the Penguin Group
Penguin Books USA Inc., 375 Hudson Street, New York, New York 10014, U.S.A
Penguin Books Ltd, 27 Wrights Lane, London W8 5TZ, England
Penguin Books Australia Ltd, Ringwood, Victoria, Australia
Penguin Books Canada Ltd, 2801 John Street, Markham, Ontario, Canada L3R
Penguin Books (N.Z.) Ltd, 182-190 Wairau Road, Auckland 10, New Zeland

Penguin Books Ltd, Registered Offices: Harmondsworth, Middlesex, England

This is an authorized reprint of a hardcover edition published by Harper
& Row, Publishers, Inc., and simultaneously in Canada by Fitzhenry &
Whiteside Limited, Toronto.

 REGISTERED TRADEMARK—MARCA REGISTRADA

LIBRARY OF CONGRESS CATALOGING-IN-PUBLICATION DATA
Twain, Mark, 1835-1910.
    The wit & wisdom of Mark Twain/edited by Alex Ayres.
        p.   cm.
    Bibliography: p.
    ISBN 0-452-01058-6
    1. Twain, Mark, 1835-1910—Quotations. I. Ayres, Alex. II. Title.
    III. Title: Wit and wisdom of Mark Twain.
PS1303.A97   1989
818'.402—dc19   88–37464 CIP

Original hardcover edition designed by Ruth Bornschlegel

First Meridian Printing, March, 1989

    4 5 6 7 8 9 10 11 12

PRINTED IN THE UNITED STATES OF AMERICA

To the ghost in the works

SOME QUOTATIONS ABOUT
MARK TWAIN

All modern American literature comes from one book by Mark Twain called *Huckleberry Finn*. American writing comes from that. There was nothing before. There has been nothing as good since.

—Ernest Hemingway, *Green Hills of*
Africa, 1935

This son of the devil, Mark Twain.

—San Francisco clergyman, 1866

I love to think of the great and godlike Clemens.

—Rudyard Kipling, letter to Frank
Doubleday, 1903

Emerson, Longfellow, Lowell, Holmes—I knew them all and the rest of our sages, poets, seers, critics, humorists; they were like one another and like other literary men; but Clemens was sole, incomparable, the Lincoln of our literature.

—William Dean Howells, *My Mark*
Twain, 1910

He was the first American author of world rank to write a genuinely colloquial and native American.

—H. L. Mencken, *The American*
Language, 1919

We are not hostile to the United States. How could I be hostile to a country that produced Mark Twain?

—S. W. R. D. Bandaranaike, prime
minister of Ceylon, 1956

Mark Twain was our greatest social critic. As such he speaks to us with an immediacy that surmounts the barriers of time.

—Philip Foner, *Mark Twain: Social Critic*, 1958

Twain was so good with crowds that he became, in competition with singers and dancers and actors and acrobats, one of the most popular performers of his time. It is so unusual, and so psychologically unlikely for a great writer to be a great performer, too, that I can think of only two similar cases—Homer's, perhaps, and Molière's.

—Kurt Vonnegut, Jr., *The Unabridged Mark Twain*, 1976

For me, of course, nothing can ever be like it again in this world. One is not likely to associate twice with a being from another star.

—Albert Bigelow Paine, *Mark Twain: A Biography*, 1912

ACKNOWLEDGMENTS

Thanks to Mark Twain, Dr. Natalie Wilson, Dr. Bruce Goldberg, Edward J. Willi of the Mark Twain Foundation, Josh Henson, Hy Cohen, Irv Levey, Hugh Van Dusen, three generations of brilliant Mark Twain scholars, and Harper & Row, Mark Twain's principal publisher, for various kinds of help with various incarnations of this work. And thanks to you, the reader, for keeping Mark Twain—and all of us in the book trade—alive.

A.A.

EXPLANATORY NOTE

Some of Mark Twain's works were not published until after his death in 1910; some have not yet been published. The quotations referenced in this book are generally dated by the year of first known publication; those dated after 1910 are posthumous. However, quotations from Mark Twain's notebooks are dated by the year of writing and quotations from Mark Twain's speeches are dated by the year of delivery. Chapter numbers rather than page numbers are cited in many instances because there are numerous editions of Mark Twain's works in print; page numbers vary from edition to edition, whereas chapter numbers remain the same. Page numbers are cited when alternative sources may be difficult or impossible to find.

The reports of my death are greatly exaggerated.

—*Mark Twain*

THE WIT & WISDOM OF MARK TWAIN

ADAM

It all began with Adam. He was the first man to tell a joke—or a lie. "How lucky Adam was," Mark Twain wrote enviously in his notebook in 1867. "He knew when he said a good thing, nobody had said it before."

Adam was not alone in the Garden of Eden, however, and does not deserve all the credit; much is due to Eve, the first woman, and Satan, the first consultant.

Adam was but human—this explains it all. He did not want the apple for the apple's sake, he wanted it only because it was forbidden. The mistake was in not forbidding the serpent; then he would have eaten the serpent.

—*Pudd'nhead Wilson*, 1894, ch. 2

Adam was the author of sin, and I wish he had taken out an international copyright on it.

—Notebook, 1877

What I cannot help wishing is that Adam and Eve had been postponed, and Martin Luther and Joan of Arc put in their place— that splendid pair equipped with temperaments not made of butter, but of asbestos. By neither sugary persuasions nor by hell fire could Satan have beguiled *them* to eat the apple.

—"The Turning Point of My Life,"
essay, 1910

Adam and Eve had many advantages, but the principal one was that they escaped teething.

—*Pudd'nhead Wilson,* 1894, ch. 4

Adam and Eve entered the world naked and unashamed—naked and pure-minded; and no descendant of theirs has ever entered it otherwise. All have entered it naked, unashamed, and clean in mind. They have entered it modest. They had to acquire immodesty and the soiled mind; there was no other way to get it.

—Satan, in DeVoto, *Letters from the Earth,* 1962, Letter 3

After all these years, I see that I was mistaken about Eve in the beginning; it is better to live outside the Garden with her than inside it without her.

—Adam, in "Adam's Diary," story,
1893

Wheresoever she was, *there* was Eden.

—Adam at Eve's grave, in "Adam's Diary," story, 1893

ADJECTIVE

As to the Adjective: when in doubt, strike it out.

—*Pudd'nhead Wilson,* 1894, ch. 11

ADULTERY

"Thou shalt not commit adultery" is a command which makes no distinction between the following persons. They are all required to obey it: children at birth. Children in the cradle. School children. Youths and maidens. Fresh adults. Older ones. Men and women of 40. Of 50. Of 60. Of 70. Of 80. Of 90. Of 100. The command does not distribute its burden equally, and cannot. It is not hard upon the three sets of children.

> —Satan, in DeVoto, *Letters from the Earth*, 1962, Letter 8

By temperament, which is the *real* law of God, many men are goats and can't help committing adultery when they get a chance; whereas there are numbers of men who, by temperament, can keep their purity and let an opportunity go by if the woman lacks in attractiveness.

> —Satan, in DeVoto, *Letters from the Earth*, 1962, Letter 8

ADVERSITY

By trying, we can easily learn to endure adversity. Another man's, I mean.

> —*Following the Equator*, 1897, vol. 2, ch. 3

ADVERTISEMENTS BY MARK TWAIN

Mark Twain first came to fame as a lecturer in San Francisco in 1866. One reason he attracted such huge crowds was that he wrote all his own advertisements. These ads were unlike anything the public had ever seen before. Twain hit upon the novel idea of luring people in with large bold promises and then surprising them with what was written in small print. Mark Twain was in fact the originator of this modern sales technique.

"A GRAND TORCHLIGHT PROCESSION," announced the poster for Twain's first lecture, in giant, glaring letters that could

be read from across the street; then followed in small print, "may
be expected; in fact, the public are privileged to expect whatever
they please."

Here are some other advertisements of Mark Twain's:

MAGNIFICENT FIREWORKS
were in contemplation for this occasion,
but the idea has been abandoned.

—Handbill for Twain's first lecture,
San Francisco, October 2, 1866

THE CELEBRATED BEARDED WOMAN!
Is not with this Circus;

THE WONDERFUL COW WITH SIX LEGS!
Is not attached to this Menagerie;

THE IRISH GIANT! WHO STANDS
9 FEET 6 INCHES
will not be present and need not be expected.

—Handbill, 1870

The wisdom will begin to flow at 8.
The trouble will begin at 8.
The Orgies will commence at 8.

—Lines from Twain posters, 1870s

IMPROMPTU FAREWELL ADDRESS,
gotten up last week, especially for this occasion.

—Poster, San Francisco, December 1866

ADVERTISING

During his days as a journalist, the young Mark Twain once
edited a small newspaper in Missouri. A subscriber wrote in,

saying that he had found a spider in his paper and asked whether this was a sign of good or bad luck. Twain answered:

"Dear Subscriber: Finding a spider in your paper was neither good luck nor bad luck for you. The spider was merely looking over our paper to see which merchant is not advertising so that he can go to that store, spin his web across the door and lead a life of undisturbed peace ever afterward."

Many a small thing has been made large by the right kind of advertising.

—A Connecticut Yankee, 1889, ch. 22

He goes by the brand, yet imagines he goes by the flavor.

—"Concerning Tobacco," essay, 1917

LADIES AND CHILDREN NOT ADMITTED.

"There," says he, "if that line don't fetch them, I don't know Arkansaw!"

—Huckleberry Finn, 1884, ch. 22

ADVICE

It is better to give than receive—especially advice. Mark Twain was always willing to donate free advice to the needy and the unsuspecting. "It's noble to be good," he said, "and it's nobler to teach others to be good, and less trouble."

A lifetime of wisdom was summed up in Mark Twain's last public address, at the commencement of St. Timothy's School for Girls in Catonsville, Maryland, on June 9, 1909. "There are three things which I consider excellent advice," Twain told the girls in his familiar slow drawl, punctuated as always by long pauses. "First, don't smoke—to excess. Second, don't drink—to excess. Third, don't marry—to excess."

It's better to keep your mouth shut and appear stupid than to open it and remove all doubt.

—Attributed to Mark Twain and to
Abraham Lincoln

When in doubt tell the truth.

—*Following the Equator*, 1897, vol. 1, ch. 2

Tell the truth or trump—but get the trick.

—*Pudd'nhead Wilson*, 1894, ch. 1

Do not tell fish stories where the people know you; but particularly, don't tell them where they know the fish.

—Notebook, 1902

Always do right. This will gratify some people, and astonish the rest.

—Card sent to Young People's
Society, Greenpoint Presbyterian
Church, Brooklyn, 1901

Always acknowledge a fault frankly. This will throw those in authority off their guard and give you an opportunity to commit more.

—Notebook, 1902

We ought never to do wrong when people are looking.

—"A Double-Barreled Detective
Story," story, 1902

Always obey your parents, when they are present.

—"Advice to Youth," speech, 1882

If a person offend you and you are in doubt as to whether it was intentional or not, do not resort to extreme measures. Simply watch your chance and hit him with a brick.

—"Advice to Youth," speech, 1882

Do not offer a compliment and ask a favor at the same time. A compliment that is charged for is not valuable.

—Notebook, 1902

Be careless in your dress if you must, but keep a tidy soul.

—Following the Equator, 1897, vol. 1, ch. 23

Earn a character first if you can. And if you can't, assume one.

—"General Miles and the Dog,"
speech, 1907

Make it a point to do something every day that you don't want to do. This is the golden rule for acquiring the habit of doing your duty without pain.

—Following the Equator, 1897, vol. 2, ch. 22

"Rise early. It is the early bird that catches the worm." Don't be fooled by this absurd saw; I once knew a man who tried it. He got up at sunrise and a horse bit him.

—Notebook, 1867

Have a place for everything and keep the thing somewhere else; this is not advice, it is merely custom.

—Notebook, 1898

Put all your eggs in the one basket and—WATCH THAT BASKET.

—Pudd'nhead Wilson, 1894, ch 15

Let us not be too particular. It is better to have old second-hand diamonds than none at all.

—Following the Equator, 1897, vol. 1, ch. 34

Don't part with your illusions. When they are gone, you may still exist, but you have ceased to live.

—Following the Equator, 1897, vol. 2, ch. 23

It is sound judgment to put on a bold face and play your hand for a hundred times what it is worth; forty-nine times out of fifty nobody dares to "call" and you rake in the chips.

—A Connecticut Yankee, 1889, ch. 39

Let us endeavor so to live that when we come to die even the undertaker will be sorry.

—*Pudd'nhead Wilson,* 1894, ch. 6

And I wish to urge upon you this—which I think is wisdom—that if you find you can't make seventy by any but an uncomfortable road, don't you go.

—Seventieth-birthday speech, 1905

Whenever you find that you are on the side of the majority, it is time to reform—(or pause and reflect.)

—Notebook, 1904

AFFECTION

Praise is well, compliment is well, but affection—that is the last and final and most precious reward that any man can win, whether by character or achievement.

—"Affection," speech, 1907

AFFLUENCE

He is now fast rising from affluence to poverty.

—"Henry Ward Beecher's Farm,"
sketch, 1885

AFTER-DINNER SPEECHES

Mark Twain and Chauncey Depew were two of the best-known after-dinner speakers of their time. Both were accustomed to star billing, but on one occasion they were both invited to the same banquet. Mark Twain's turn came first. He spoke for twenty minutes and made a great hit with the crowd, telling several hilarious stories.

It was a hard act to follow, but Chauncey Depew stood up. "Mr. Toastmaster, Ladies and Gentlemen," the famous raconteur began. "I have a confession to make. Before this dinner, Mark Twain and I agreed to swap speeches. He has just delivered my speech, and I thank you for the fine reception you have accorded it. But I regret to say that I have lost his speech and cannot remember a thing he had to say."

With that, Chauncey Depew sat down to much applause.

AFTERLIFE

Mark Twain once attended a dinner party at which the subject of heaven and hell was raised. Throughout the heated discussion Twain said nothing. Finally, the hostess asked, "Why haven't you said something, Mr. Clemens? Surely you must have an opinion on this subject."

"Madam, you must excuse me," Mark Twain replied. "I am silent because of necessity. I have friends in both places."

Many when they come to die have spent all the truth that was in them, and enter the next world as paupers. I have saved up enough to make an astonishment there.

—Speech at Savages Club, London, 1899

Eternal Rest sounds comforting in the pulpit. . . . Well, you try it once, and see how heavy time will hang on your hands.

—"Captain Stormfield's Visit to
Heaven," story, 1907

AGE

When Mark Twain returned to Hannibal after thirty years, it seemed that the men had aged less than the women. "I saw men whom thirty years had changed but slightly," he wrote in *Life on the Mississippi*, "but their wives had grown old. These were good women; it is very wearing to be good."

Wrinkles should merely indicate where smiles have been.

—*Following the Equator*, 1897, vol. 2, ch. 16

Whatever a man's age, he can reduce it several years by putting a bright-colored flower in his button-hole.

—*The American Claimant*, 1892, ch. 20

It takes some little time to accept and realize the fact that while you have been growing old, your friends have not been standing still in that matter.

—*Life on the Mississippi*, 1883, ch. 55

Life would be infinitely happier if we could only be born at the age of eighty and gradually approach eighteen.

—Phelps, *Autobiography with Letters*, 1939, p. 965

AMBITION

Keep away from people who try to belittle your ambitions. Small people always do that, but the really great make you feel that you, too, can become great.

—MacLaren, *Morally We Roll Along*, 1938, p. 66

AMERICA

Mark Twain liked to play the role of national spokesman, defending America from the attacks of snobbish European intellectuals, who regarded America as a backward nation. In 1895, a French travel writer, Paul Bourget, made the well-publicized observation that the average American did not know who his grandfather was. Mark Twain made the famous retort that the American was still better off than the average Frenchman, who was not sure who his *father* was.

"If I look harried and worn it is not from an ill conscience," said Mark Twain in a speech "On Foreign Critics" in 1890. "It is from sitting up nights to worry about the foreign critic. He won't concede that we have a civilization, a 'real' civilization."

Real civilization began with the American Revolution, Mark Twain contended, and flowed eastward toward Europe, spreading the New World ideals of freedom, equality, enterprise and innovation. Twain did not consider the European monarchies to be truly civilized, and he mocked their cultural pretensions in his irreverent travel books.

"There are some partial civilizations scattered around over Europe. Pretty lofty civilizations they are, too. But who begot them? What is the seed from which they sprang? Liberty and intelligence. What planted that seed? There are dates and statistics which suggest it was the American Revolution that planted it," he said in his 1890 Independence Day speech. "We hoisted the banner of revolution and raised the first genuine shout for human liberty that had ever been heard."

Twain also liked to play the role of national critic, chiding Americans to live up to their noble national ideals. He was particularly critical of politicians. He wrote in *Pudd'nhead Wilson's New Calendar,* "It could probably be shown by facts and figures that there is no distinctly native American criminal class except Congress."

But despite his criticism of American government and particularly American foreign policy, Mark Twain remained to the end a champion of American civilization. In 1897, soon after he sent his famous cable from London saying, "The reports of my death are greatly exaggerated," he wrote home to a friend in Hartford: "As far as I can see, nothing remains to be reported, except that I have become a foreigner. When you hear it, don't you believe it. And don't take the trouble to deny it. Merely just raise the American flag on our house in Hartford, and let it talk."

It is by the goodness of God that in our country we have those three unspeakably precious things: freedom of speech, freedom of conscience, and the prudence never to practice either of them.

—*Following the Equator,* 1897, vol. 1, ch. 20

We are called the nation of inventors. And we are. We could still claim that title and wear its loftiest honors if we had stopped with the first thing we ever invented, which was human liberty.

—"Foreign Critics," speech, 1890

I should like to say that we are a faultless people but I am restrained by recollection. I know several persons who have erred and transgressed—to put it plainly, they have done wrong. I have heard still of others—of a number of persons, in fact—who are not perfect.

—"The Watermelon," speech, 1907

When it comes down to pure ornamental cursing, the native American is gifted above the sons of men.

—*Roughing It,* 1872, ch. 60

I think that the reason why we Americans seem to be so addicted to trying to get rich suddenly is merely because the *opportunity* to make promising efforts in that direction has offered itself to us with a frequency all out of proportion to the European experience.

—"What Paul Bourget Thinks of Us,"
essay, 1895

In Boston they ask, How much does he know? In New York, How much is he worth? In Philadelphia, Who were his parents?

—"What Paul Bourget Thinks of Us,"
essay, 1895

Ours is the "land of the free"—nobody denies that—nobody challenges it. (Maybe it is because we won't let other people testify.)

—*Roughing It,* 1872, ch. 54
(commenting on mistreatment of
Chinese in the West)

AMERICANS

Asked the difference between the Englishman and the American, Mark Twain gave this answer:

"An Englishman is a person who does things because they have been done before. An American is a person who does things because they haven't been done before."

ANCESTORS

Mark Twain was irritated by people who boasted about their ancestry. Once when an ancestor-worshiper inquired about the Clemens family tree, Mark Twain heaved a heavy sigh and said sadly, "My grandfather was cut down in the prime of his life." He paused momentously as if gathering strength for a long, tearful tale, then added: "My grandmother always used to tell us that if he had been cut down fifteen minutes earlier, he could have been resuscitated."

I was never able to persuade myself to call a gibbet by its right name when accounting for other ancestors of mine, but always spoke of it as the "platform"—puerilely intimating that they were out lecturing when it happened.

—*Christian Science*, 1907, bk. 2, ch. 1

My first American ancestor, gentlemen, was an Indian—an early Indian. Your ancestors skinned him alive, and I am an orphan. . . . All those Salem witches were ancestors of mine. Your people made it tropical for them. . . . The first slave brought into New England out of Africa by your progenitors was an ancestor of mine—for I am a mixed breed, an infinitely shaded and exquisite Mongrel.

—"Plymouth Rock and the Pilgrims,"
speech, 1881

ANGELS

I have traveled more than anyone else, and I have noticed that even the angels speak English with an accent.

—*Following the Equator*, 1897, vol. 2,
conclusion

I have been on the verge of being an angel all my life, but it's never happened yet.

—Paine, *Mark Twain: A Biography*,
1912, vol. 2, p. 1010

ANGER

Anger, according to Sigmund Freud, was a frequent theme in Mark Twain's humor. In *Jokes and Their Relation to the Unconscious*, Freud gives an example from a Twain lecture:

"Mark Twain describes how his brother constructed a subterranean dwelling, into which he brought a bed, a table and a lamp and which he roofed over with a large piece of sailcloth with a hole in the middle. At night, however, after the hut was finished, a cow that was being driven home fell through the opening of the roof on to the table and put out the lamp. His brother patiently helped to get the beast out and put the establishment to rights again. Next night the same interruption was repeated and his brother behaved as before. And so it was every following night. Repetition makes the story comic, but Mark Twain ends it by reporting that on the forty-sixth night, when the cow fell through again, his brother finally remarked: 'The thing's beginning to get monotonous.'

"At this our humorous pleasure cannot be kept back," Freud explained, "for what we had long expected to hear was that this obstinate set of misfortunes would make his brother *angry.*"

When angry, count four; when very angry, swear.

—*Pudd'nhead Wilson,* 1894, ch. 10

ANIMALS

It is just like man's vanity and impertinence to call an animal dumb because it is dumb to his dull perceptions.

—"What Is Man?" essay, 1906

Of all the animals, man is the only one that is cruel. He is the only one that inflicts pain for the pleasure of doing it.

—"The Lowest Animal," essay, 1897

ANNIVERSARY

What ought to be done to the man who invented the celebrating of anniversaries? Mere killing would be too light.

—Notebook, 1896

APPRENTICESHIP

Even Noah got no salary for the first six months—partly on account of the weather and partly because he was learning navigation.

—DeVoto, *Mark Twain in Eruption,* 1940, p. 165

APPROVAL

We can secure other people's approval if we do right and try hard·
but our own is worth a hundred of it, and no way has been found
out of securing that.

—Following the Equator, 1897, vol. 1, ch. 14

ARGUMENT

Women cannot receive even the most palpably judicious sugges-
tion without arguing it; that is, married women.

—"Experience of the McWilliamses,"
story, 1875

There is nothing like instances to grow hair on a bald-headed
argument.

—Unpublished manuscript on British
copyright law

ARISTOCRACY

Any kind of royalty, however modified, *any* kind of aristocracy,
however pruned, is rightly an insult.

—A Connecticut Yankee, 1009, ch. 8

The blunting effects of slavery upon the slaveholder's moral perceptions are known and conceded, the world over, and a privileged class, an aristocracy, is but a band of slaveholders under
another name.

—A Connecticut Yankee, 1889, ch. 25

We have to be despised by somebody whom we regard as above
us or we are not happy; we have to have somebody to worship
and envy or we cannot be content. In America we manifest this
in all the ancient and customary ways. In public we scoff at titles
and hereditary privilege but privately we hanker after them, and
when we get a chance we buy them for cash and a daughter.

—DeVoto, *Mark Twain in Eruption,*
1940, p. 64

ARK

Oh, this infernal Human Race! I wish I had it in the Ark again—
with an auger!

—"In Memory of Samuel Langhorn
Clemens," 1922, p. 37
(American Academy of Arts and
Letters pamphlet)

ARMS RACE

By and by when each nation has 20,000 battleships and 5,000,000
soldiers we shall all be safe and the wisdom of statesmanship will
stand confirmed.

—Notebook, 1902

ART

Mark Twain once called upon the painter Whistler in his studio
and, absorbed in conversation, absentmindedly reached out to
touch one of the freshly painted canvases.

"Don't touch that!" exclaimed Whistler. "Don't you see it
isn't dry yet?"

"Oh, I don't mind," said Twain, good-naturedly. "I have
gloves on."

Can it be possible that the painters make John the Baptist a
Spaniard in Madrid and an Irishman in Dublin?

—*Innocents Abroad*, 1869, ch. 19

A good legible label is usually worth, for information, a ton of
significant attitude and expression in a historical picture.

—*Life on the Mississippi*, 1883, ch. 44

It looked natural because it looked somehow as if it were in pain.

—Description of a Phidias sculpture

A tortoise-shell cat having a fit in a platter of tomatoes . . .

—Description of Turner's painting *The
Slave Ship*

ARTISTIC LICENSE

Criticism is a queer thing. If I print, "She was stark naked" and then proceeded to describe her person in detail, what critic would not howl? Who would venture to leave the book on a parlor table? But the artist does this and all ages gather around and look and talk and point.

—Notebook, 1879

ASS

Concerning the difference between man and the jackass: some observers hold that there isn't any. But this wrongs the jackass.

—Notebook, 1898

There is no character, howsoever good and fine, but it can be destroyed by ridicule, howsoever poor and witless. Observe the ass, for instance: his character is about perfect, he is the choicest spirit among all the humbler animals, yet see what ridicule has brought him to. Instead of feeling complimented when we are called an ass, we are left in doubt.

—*Pudd'nhead Wilson*, 1894, preface

AUTOGRAPH

"Writing is my trade and I exercise it only when I am obliged to," Mark Twain once replied to a written request for an autograph. "It would never be fair to ask a doctor for one of his corpses to remember him by."

AUTHORS

"I was sorry to have my name mentioned as one of the great authors," said Mark Twain in a speech in London in 1899 after a flattering introduction, "because they have a sad habit of dying off. Chaucer is dead, Spenser is dead, so is Milton, so is Shakespeare, and I am not feeling very well myself."

I have been an author for 20 years and an ass for 55.

—Letter to unknown person, 1890

AUTHORSHIP

The elderly owner of a roadside stand in Hannibal, Missouri, was asked if he had known Mark Twain as a boy.

"Sure, I knew him," the old geezer replied indignantly. "And I know just as many stories as he did, too. Only difference is, he writ 'em down."

Authorship is not a Trade, it is an inspiration; Authorship does not keep an Office, its habitation is all out under the sky, and everywhere the winds are blowing and the sun is shining and the creatures of God are free. Now then, since I have no Trade and keep no Office, I am not taxable under Schedule D, section 14.

—"A Petition to the Queen of
England," 1887
(plea for exemption from English tax
on royalties)

BABIES

One of Mark Twain's most triumphant speeches, "The Babies," was delivered in 1879 at a banquet in honor of Ulysses S. Grant. The last of a long series of speakers, Mark Twain stepped to the platform at three o'clock in the morning and roused a weary crowd by toasting "the babies."

"We haven't all had the good fortune to be ladies; we haven't all been generals, or poets, or statesmen; but when the toast works down to the babies, we stand on common ground," he began.

Babies are national treasures, he told the audience. "Among the three or four million cradles now rocking in the land are some which this nation would preserve for ages as sacred things, if we could but know which ones they are."

But he warned his listeners never to underestimate a baby on account of his small size. "He is enterprising, irrepressible, and brimful of lawless activities. Do what you please, you can't make him stay on the reservation."

Mark Twain offered this advice to prospective parents. "As long as you are in your right mind don't you ever pray for twins. Twins amount to a permanent riot. And there ain't no real difference between triplets and an insurrection."

A baby is an inestimable blessing and bother.

—Letter to Annie Webster, 1876

BAGGAGE HANDLERS

At Union Station in Washington, D.C., Mark Twain asked a baggage handler, "Is that satchel strong enough to go in the baggage car?"

The baggage handler lifted the satchel above his head and hurled it to the pavement with all his might. "That," he declared, "is what it will get in Philadelphia." Then the baggage man picked up the bag and smashed it against the side of the car five or six times. "That," said he, "is what it will get in Chicago." Next he heaved the bag up in the air as high as he could toss it, and when it landed, jumped up and down on it repeatedly. "And that," he said, "is what it will get in Sioux City."

The baggage man paused, looked up at Mark Twain and added: "And if you are going any further than Sioux City, you'd better take it in the Pullman with you."

BALDNESS

During his "Roughing It" days in Nevada, Mark Twain made the acquaintance of Bill Nye, later the governor of Nevada, a man who was a paragon of baldness. "He was the baldest human being I ever saw," Mark Twain wrote in his autobiography. "His whole skull was brilliantly shining. It was like a dome with the sun flashing upon it." Once somebody expressed astonishment at his extraordinary baldness. "You should see my brother," replied Bill Nye.

One day, Twain recalled, Bill Nye fell overboard from a ferryboat and when he came up for air a woman's voice broke high over the tumult of frightened and anxious exclamations and said, "You shameless thing! And ladies present! Go down and come up the other way."

BANKER

A banker is a fellow who lends you his umbrella when the sun is shining and wants it back the minute it begins to rain.

—Attributed

BANKRUPTCY

Soon after Mark Twain bought a publishing house, a friend bumped into him and asked him how he was.

"Splendid!" replied Twain enthusiastically. "I was fortunate to be let in on the ground floor!"

Some time later, after the publishing firm went bankrupt, the same friend bumped into Twain again, and hearing the sad news, inquired, "What happened? You told me you were let in on the ground floor!"

"So I was," answered Mark Twain. "But there was a son-of-a-bitch in the basement!"

BANQUET

A banquet is probably the most fatiguing thing in the world except ditchdigging.

—"Last Visit to England," in DeVoto,
Mark Twain in Eruption, 1940

BARBER

Mark Twain once had a close shave with an overly talkative barber. When the garrulous barber had finished the shave, he ran his hand across his customer's chin and, holding up the razor, said: "Shall I go over it again?"

"No," replied Mark Twain wearily, "I heard every damned word."

BARNUM, P. T.

Mark Twain was amused by P. T. Barnum's aggressive advertising methods and made light of them in "The Stolen White Elephant" (1882). In this story, a gigantic white Siamese elephant runs on a wild rampage through upper New York State, wreaking havoc and destruction in one village after another while a group of dedicated detectives, led by the celebrated Inspector Blunt, try to track the elephant down. When P. T. Barnum gets wind of this, he offers $4,000 a year for the exclusive privilege of using the elephant as a "traveling advertising medium from now till detectives find him." Inspector Blunt haggles Barnum to $7,000 and the deal is sealed. Shortly afterward, the inspector receives this telegram from one of his detectives, in Baxter Center, New York:

ELEPHANT BEEN HERE, PLASTERED OVER WITH CIRCUS BILLS, AND BROKE UP A REVIVAL, STRIKING DOWN AND DAMAGING MANY WHO WERE ON THE POINT OF ENTERING UPON A BETTER LIFE.

BEAUTY

One is apt to overestimate beauty when it is rare.

—*Innocents Abroad,* 1869, ch. 51

In true beauty, more depends upon right location and judicious distribution of feature than upon multiplicity of them. So also as regards color. The very combination of colors which in a volcanic eruption would add beauty to a landscape might detach it from a girl.

—*The American Claimant,* 1892, ch. 5

One frequently only finds out how really beautiful a really beautiful woman is after considerable acquaintance with her; and the rule applies to Niagara Falls, to majestic mountains, and to mosques—especially to mosques.

—*Innocents Abroad,* 1869, ch. 54

There are women who have an indefinable charm in their faces which makes them beautiful to their intimates, but a cold stranger who tried to reason the matter out and find this beauty would fail.

—*A Tramp Abroad,* 1880, vol. 2, ch. 19

BEGGARS

We are all beggars, each in his own way.

—Paine, *Mark Twain: A Biography*, 1912, vol. 3, p. 1421

BELIEFS

If the man doesn't believe as we do, we say he is a crank, and that settles it. I mean, it does nowadays, because now we can't burn him.

—*Following the Equator*, 1897, vol. 2, ch. 17

The easy confidence with which I know another man's religion is folly teaches me to suspect that my own is also.

—Paine, *Mark Twain: A Biography*, 1912, vol. 3, p. 1584

We despise all reverences and all objects of reverence which are outside the pale of our list of sacred things. And yet, with strange inconsistency, we are shocked when other people despise and defile the things which are holy to us.

—*Following the Equator*, 1897, vol. 2, ch. 17

Between believing a thing and thinking you *know* is only a small step and quickly taken.

—"3,000 Years Among the Microbes," story, 1905

In religion and politics people's beliefs and convictions are in almost every case gotten at second-hand, and without examination.

—Neider, *Autobiography*, 1959, ch. 78

My land, the power of training! Of influence! Of education! It can bring a body up to believe anything.

—*A Connecticut Yankee*, 1889, ch. 21

BIBLE

Mark Twain, the most irreverent of writers, was actually a very religious man, but he did not subscribe to any orthodox set of beliefs, and he did not believe that the Bible was literally the word of God. He once said, "It ain't those parts of the Bible that I can't understand that bother me, it is the parts that I do understand."

It is full of interest. It has noble poetry in it; and some clever fables; and some blood-drenched history; and some good morals; and a wealth of obscenity; and upwards of a thousand lies.

—Satan, in DeVoto, *Letters from the
Earth,* 1962, Letter 3

The two Testaments are interesting, each in its own way. The Old one gives us a picture of these people's Deity as he was before he got religion, the other one gives us a picture of him as he appeared afterward.

—Satan, in DeVoto, *Letters from the
Earth,* 1962, Letter 10

The Christian's Bible is a drug store. Its contents remain the same; but the medical practice changes.

—"Bible Teaching and Religious
Practice," essay, 1923

BICYCLING

In the spring of 1884, the bicycle, in its primitive high-wheeler form, was just coming into vogue. Mark Twain was always fascinated with new inventions, and at the age of forty-nine he resolved to learn how to ride the bicycle. He even took lessons with a young German instructor. His efforts were not always successful, but he seemed to have a natural aptitude for dismounting. "Although wholly inexperienced, I dismounted in the best time on record," he wrote proudly.

His instructor, however, regarded him as a hopeless case, and said, "Mr. Clemens, it's remarkable—you can fall off the bicycle in more ways than the man that invented it."

One incident, described in "Taming the Bicycle," illustrates the hazards of being Mark Twain's bicycle instructor: "We got up a handsome speed, and presently traversed a brick, and I went out over the top of the tiller and landed, head down, on the instruc-

tor's back, and saw the machine fluttering in the air between me
and the sun. It was well it came down on us, for that broke the
fall, and it was not injured."

Mark Twain used to claim that he invented all the new bicycle
profanity that has since come into general use.

Get a bicycle. You will not regret it. If you live.

—"Taming the Bicycle," essay, 1917

BIRTH

Why is it that we rejoice at a birth and grieve at a funeral? It is
because we are not the person involved.

—Pudd'nhead Wilson, 1894, ch. 9

BLASPHEMY

When Mark Twain was a young apprentice printer in Hannibal,
he was once severely chastised by the local minister, who over-
heard him say, "Great God!"

"Why commit the Unforgiven Sin when Great Scott would
have done as well?" the minister exhorted him.

Some time later, the minister arranged to have one of his
sermons printed in a pamphlet. The task of correcting the proofs
fell to young Mark Twain at the printshop. Remembering the
minister's admonition, Twain revised the Reverend's text, correcting "Great God" to "Great Scott" and "Father, Son and Holy
Ghost" to "Father, Son and Caesar's Ghost."

BOASTS

Boasting has always been the cheapest form of advertising. In
certain societies it has even achieved the status of a sport. Boasting was one of the principal pastimes on the American frontier,
and the "tall talk" of "ring-tailed roarers" is a part of American
folk history. Mark Twain recognized this boasting as a peculiar art
form which, at its most inspired, approached poetry. He made this
tall talk a permanent part of American literature by recording

some samples of it in the third chapter of *Life on the Mississippi*. He described a contest between two boasters.

"Sired by a hurricane, dam'd by an earthquake, half-brother to the cholera, nearly related to the small pox on my mother's side," said one. "Blood's my natural drink, and the wails of the dying is music to my ear! Cast your eye on me, gentlemen!—and lay low and hold your breath, for I'm 'bout to turn myself loose!"

"I'm a child of sin, *don't* let me get a start!" said the other. "Smoked glass, here, for all! Don't attempt to look at me with the naked eye, gentlemen! When I'm playful I use the meridians and parallels of latitude for a seine, and drag the Atlantic Ocean for whales! I scratch my head with the lightning and purr myself to sleep with the thunder!"

BODY

Whose property is my body? Probably mine. I so regard it. If I experiment with it, who must be answerable? I, not the State. If I choose injudiciously, does the State die? Oh, no.

—"Osteopathy," speech, 1901

BOOKS

"The man who does not read good books has no advantage over the man who can't read them," declared Mark Twain, who had definite opinions about what books were good and what books were not.

"There are many sorts of books," he told a young audience in a speech delivered in 1882. "But good ones are the sort for the young to read. Remember that. They are a great, an inestimable, an unspeakable means of improvement. Therefore be careful in your selection, my young friends. Be very careful. Confine yourselves exclusively to Robertson's Sermons, Baxter's *Saint's Rest, The Innocents Abroad,* and works of that kind."

"Classic." A book which people praise and don't read.

—*Following the Equator,* 1897, vol. 1, ch. 25

Pilgrim's Progress, about a man that left his family, it didn't say why.

—*Huckleberry Finn*, 1884, ch. 17
(Huck's interpretation)

It seems to me that *Deerslayer* is just simply a literary *delirium tremens*.

—"Fenimore Cooper's Literary
Offenses," essay, 1895

When I am king, they shall not have bread and shelter only, but also teachings out of books, for a full belly is little worth where the mind is starved.

—*The Prince and the Pauper*, 1882, ch. 4

BORROWING

A visitor to Mark Twain's house in Hartford observed mountains of books stacked on the floor.

The author apologized for the disorder. "But you see," he lamented, "it is so very difficult to borrow shelves."

For Mark Twain, borrowing was a more convenient and economical means of acquiring property than buying. But his friends and neighbors soon grew wary of him. When he once asked a neighbor if he could borrow a certain book, the neighbor, aware of Twain's reputation as a notorious book-borrower, replied archly, "Why, certainly, Mr. Clemens, you are welcome to read it. But I must ask you to read it here. I make it a rule never to let a book leave my library."

A few weeks later, the same neighbor asked if he could borrow Mark Twain's lawn mower.

"Why, certainly," was Twain's answer. "You're welcome to use it. But I must ask you to use it here. I make it a rule never to let my lawn mower leave my lawn."

BOSTON

Tomorrow night I appear for the first time before a Boston audience—4000 critics.

—Letter to his sister, Pamela Clemens
Moffet, 1867

BOYHOOD

Mark Twain claimed that during his boyhood on the Mississippi he had no fewer than nine narrow escapes from drowning. One time he was pulled from a hole in Bear Creek and brought home in a sad, soggy condition. Neighbors were alarmed, but his mother took it calmly. After the boy was drained out, inflated, and set going again, she was heard to remark, "I don't suppose there was much danger. People born to be hanged are safe in water."

BOYS

The Adventures of Tom Sawyer is probably the greatest novel ever written about boyhood in America. But it is not the story of a good little boy. Mark Twain is quick to point out that his hero is not the model boy:

"He was not the model boy of the village. He knew the model boy very well—and loathed him."

Every village had its model boy, of course, and the model boy in the novel was modeled after the model boy Mark Twain had known in Hannibal.

In *Life on the Mississippi,* Twain recalls him. "The Model Boy of my time—we never had but the one—was perfect; perfect in manners, perfect in dress, perfect in conduct, perfect in filial piety, perfect in exterior godliness . . . he was the admiration of all the mothers and the detestation of all their sons."

When Twain returned to Hannibal in 1883 to gather background material for *Life on the Mississippi,* he inquired about the fate of his various boyhood acquaintances, including the model boy. "I was told what became of him, but as it was a disappointment to me, I will not enter into details. He succeeded in life."

There comes a time in every rightly constructed boy's life when he has a raging desire to go somewhere and dig for hidden treasure.

—Attributed

Now and then we had a hope that if we lived and were good, God would permit us to be pirates.

—*Life on the Mississippi,* 1883, ch. 4

I can see that marching company yet and I can almost feel again the consuming desire I had to join it. But they had no use for boys twelve and thirteen, and before I had a chance in another war, the desire to kill people to whom I had not been introduced had passed away

—Neider, *Autobiography*, 1959, ch. 15

We were good Presbyterian boys when the weather was doubtful. When it was fair we did wander a little from the fold.

—"I Have Tried to Do Good," speech, 1902

Each boy has one or two sensitive spots and if you can find out where they are located you have only to touch them and you can scorch him as with fire.

—Neider, *Autobiography*, 1959, ch. 9

A boy's life is not all comedy; much of the tragic enters into it.

—Neider, *Autobiography*, 1959, ch. 9

Schoolboy days are no happier than the days of afterlife, but we look back upon them regretfully because we have forgotten our punishments at school and how we grieved when our marbles were lost and our kites destroyed—because we have forgotten all the sorrows and privations of that canonized epoch and remember only its orchard robberies, its wooden-sword pageants, and its fishing holidays.

—*Innocents Abroad*, 1869, ch. 54

BRAVERY

To believe yourself brave is to *be* brave; it is the one only essential thing.

—*Joan of Arc*, 1896, bk. 2, ch. 11

BROTHERHOOD

The universal brotherhood of man is our most precious possession, what there is of it.

—*Following the Equator*, 1897, vol. 1, ch. 27

BROTHERS

In *The Adventures of Tom Sawyer,* the hero gets into a name-calling contest with another boy. The classic dialogue runs like this:

"You're a coward and a pup. I'll tell my big brother on you, and he can thrash you with his little finger, and I'll make him do it, too."

"What do I care for your big brother? I've got a brother that's bigger than he is—and what's more, he can throw him over that fence, too." (Both brothers were imaginary.)

BUSINESS

"To succeed in business, avoid my example," Mark Twain told a *New York Times* reporter in 1901. Actually, few writers in history have had so much firsthand experience in business ventures. In addition to the millions he made from selling his own books by subscription, his marketing successes included a scrapbook he invented and one of the first photographic albums. His failures included the Paige typesetter, a device he invented to keep children from falling out of bed, a cure-all called Plasmon, and a board game he finally conceded was so complicated that nobody would learn how to play it unless he was present to explain all the rules. Twain made and lost several fortunes during his checkered career as a businessman, but in the end he always made good. After his publishing company went bankrupt in 1894, he was able to pay back his creditors one hundred cents on the dollar within four years.

There are two times in a man's life when he should not speculate: when he can't afford it, and when he can.

—*Following the Equator,* 1897, vol. 2, ch. 20

October. This is one of the peculiarly dangerous months to speculate in stocks in. The others are July, January, September, April, November, May, March, June, December, August, and February.

—*Pudd'nhead Wilson,* 1894, ch. 13

For business reasons, I must preserve the outward signs of sanity.

—Letter to William T. Stead, 1890

A man pretty much always refuses another man's first offer, no matter what it is.

—*The Gilded Age*, 1873, ch. 6

It is no use to throw a good thing away merely because the market isn't ripe yet.

—*A Connecticut Yankee*, 1889, ch. 4

Beautiful credit! The foundation of modern society.

—*The Gilded Age*, 1873, ch. 26

I wonder how much it would take to buy a soap-bubble, if there was only one in the world.

—*A Tramp Abroad*, 1880, vol. 2, ch. 13

No one with a specialty can hope to have a monopoly of it.

—*A Tramp Abroad*, 1880, vol. 1, ch. 16

Let your secret sympathies and your compassion be always with the under dog in the fight this is magnanimity; but bet on the other one—this is business.

—Paine, *Mark Twain: A Biography*, 1912, vol. 2, p. 705

Prosperity is the best protector of principle.

—*Following the Equator*, 1897, vol. 2, ch. 2

The low level which commercial morality has reached in America is deplorable. We have humble God fearing Christian men among us who will stoop to do things for a million dollars that they ought not to be willing to do for less than 2 millions.

—Notebook, 1902

CAIN

Mark Twain originally dedicated *Roughing It* to Cain, but was persuaded by his publishers to replace that Cain-raising dedication with a more tasteful one. This is the wording of the deleted dedication, which is as timely today as ever:

To the Late Cain
This Book Is Dedicated

Not on account of respect for his memory, for it merits little respect; not on account of sympathy for him, for his bloody deed places him without the pale of sympathy, strictly speaking, but out of a mere human commiseration for him; in that it was his misfortune to live in a dark age that knew not the beneficent insanity plea.

CARNEGIE, ANDREW

Mark Twain once wrote a letter to Andrew Carnegie, asking for money. The letter later found its way into the newspapers.

> Dear Sir & Friend:
>
> You seem to be in prosperity. Could you lend an admirer $1.50 to buy a hymn-book with? I will bless you. God will bless you—I feel it; I know it—and it will do a great deal of good.
>
> > Yours Truly,
> > Mark Twain
>
> P.S. Don't send the hymn-book; send the money; I want to make the selection myself.

Carnegie wrote back in reply: "Nothing less than a two-dollar and a half hymn-book *gilt* will do for you. Your place in the choir (celestial) demands that and you shall have it."

CATS

Mark Twain was a passionate lover of cats, and this enthusiasm was shared by the rest of his family. Cats were always a major topic of discussion in the Clemens household. Once, when he was away on a lecture tour, Twain wrote playfully to his young daughter Susy: "I saw a cat yesterday with 4 legs—and yet it was only a yellow cat, and rather small, too, for its size. They were not *all* fore legs—several of them were hind legs; indeed almost a majority of them were."

A cat is more intelligent than people believe, and can be taught any crime.

—Notebook, 1895

A home without a cat—and a well-fed, well-petted and properly revered cat—may be a perfect home, perhaps, but how can it prove title?

—*Pudd'nhead Wilson*, 1894, ch. 1

If man could be crossed with a cat, it would improve man, but it would deteriorate the cat.

—Notebook, 1894

One of the striking differences between a cat and a lie is that a cat has only nine lives.

—*Pudd'nhead Wilson,* 1894, ch. 1

CENSORSHIP

Huckleberry Finn was attacked by righteous book-banners when it was first published in the United States, in 1885, and a hundred years later it was still being banned periodically from libraries and reading lists at some schools—including, ironically, Mark Twain Intermediate School in Fairfax, Virginia, where a curriculum committee pronounced the book "racist."

In the centennial year of *Huckleberry Finn*'s publication, the President of the United States joined in the literary controversy. The conservative Ronald Reagan defended the book in a speech before the National Association of Independent Schools, saying it teaches a "hatred of bigotry."

"Huck works hard to keep Jim free, and in the end he succeeds," affirmed President Reagan. "I believe the book says much about the moral aims of education—about the qualities of heart that we seek to impart to our children." But the century-old censorship debate goes on.

When a Brooklyn library banished *Huckleberry Finn* and *Tom Sawyer* from the children's room in 1905, a dissenting librarian wrote privately to Mark Twain. This is Twain's response, which was not published until after his death:

> Dear Sir: I am greatly troubled by what you say. I wrote *Tom Sawyer* and *Huck Finn* for adults exclusively, and it always distresses me when I find that boys and girls have been allowed access to them. The mind that becomes soiled in youth can never again be washed clean. I know this by my own experience, and to this day I cherish an unappeasable bitterness against the unfaithful guardians of my young life, who not only permitted but compelled me to read an unexpurgated Bible through before I was 15 years old. None can do that and ever draw a clean, sweet breath again this side of the grave. . . .
>
> Most honestly do I wish that I could say a softening word or two in defense of Huck's character since you wish

it, but really, in my opinion, it is no better than those of Solomon, David, and the rest of the sacred brotherhood.

The Committee of the Public Library of Concord, Mass. have given us a rattling tip-top puff which will go into every paper in the country. They have expelled Huck from their library as "trash and suitable only for the slums." That will sell 25,000 copies for us for sure.

—Letter to publisher Charles
Webster, 1885

CHANGE

Change is the handmaiden Nature requires to do her miracles with.

—*Roughing It,* 1872, ch. 56

What, then, is the true Gospel of consistency? Change.

—"Consistency," speech, 1887

CHARITY

When he was testifying before Congress in support of the new copyright bill on December 6, 1906, Mark Twain concluded his speech with this homily on human charity:

I do seem to have an extraordinary interest in a whole lot of arts and things. The bill is full of those that I have nothing to do with. But that is in line with my generous, liberal nature. I can't help it. I feel toward those same people the same wide *charity* felt by the man who arrived at home at two o'clock in the morning from the club and was feeling so perfectly satisfied with life, so happy, and so comfortable, and there was his house weaving and weaving and weaving around. So he watched his chance, and by and by when the steps got in his neighborhood he made a jump and climbed up on the portico.

And the house went on weaving and weaving and weaving, but he watched the door, and when it came around his way he plunged through it. He got to the stairs, and when he went up on all fours the house was so unsteady that he could hardly reach the top step; his toe hitched on that step, and of course he crumpled all down and rolled all the way down the stairs, and fetched up at the bottom with his arm around the newel post, and he said, "God pity the poor sailors out at sea on a night like this!"

Remember the poor—it costs nothing.

—Attributed

In all the ages, three-fourths of the support of the great charities has been conscience money.

—"A Humane Word from Satan," essay, 1905

CHASTITY

Chastity—it can be carried too far.

—Speech at a dinner for Andrew Carnegie, 1906

CHEER

The best way to cheer yourself is to try to cheer somebody else up.

—Notebook, 1896

CHICAGO

SATAN (impatiently) to NEW-COMER. The trouble with you Chicago people is that you think you are the best people down here; whereas you are merely the most numerous.

—*Following the Equator*, 1897, vol. 2, ch. 24

CHILDREN

Familiarity breeds contempt—and children.

—Notebook, 1894

The proverb says that Providence protects children and idiots. This is really true. I know it because I have tested it.

—Neider, *Autobiography*, 1959, ch. 26

We have nine children, now—half boys and half girls.

—Eve's Diary, in "Papers of the Adam Family," *Letters from the Earth*, 1962

It is a shameful thing to insult a little child. It has its feelings, it has its small dignity; and since it cannot defend them, it is surely an ignoble act to injure them.

—"Which Was the Dream?" story, 1897

Children have but little charity for one another's defects.

—Neider, *Autobiography*, 1959, ch. 4

We are always too busy for our children; we never give them the time or interest they deserve. We lavish gifts upon them; but the most precious gift—our personal association, which means so much to them—we give grudgingly.

—Paine, *Mark Twain: A Biography*, 1912, vol. 3, p. 1299

Part of my plan has been to pleasantly remind adults of what they were themselves, and of how they felt and thought and talked, and what queer enterprises they sometimes engaged in.

—*Tom Sawyer*, 1876, preface

CHINA

Once civilized, China can never be uncivilized again.

—"The United States of Lyncherdom," essay, 1923

The Chinese are universally conceded to be excellent people, honest, honorable, illustrious, trustworthy, kind-hearted, and all that—leave them alone, they are plenty good enough just as they are; and besides, almost every convert runs a risk of catching our civilization.

—"The United States of
Lyncherdom," essay, 1923

CHRIST

There has been only one Christian. They caught and crucified him—early.

—Notebook, 1898

If Christ were here now, there is one thing he would *not* be—a Christian.

—Notebook, 1897

CHRISTIANITY

Mark Twain went to Hawaii as a newspaper correspondent in 1866 and there he gathered the material for the lecture on "The Sandwich Islands" that launched his career. In that lecture, he described an unforgettable interview with the king of the Sandwich Islands. When the conversation turned to religion, the king assured Twain that the natives understood the true meaning of the Christian sacrament. "We understand Christianity," said the king. "We have eaten the missionaries."

The serene confidence of a Christian with four aces . . .

—Walker, *The Washoe Giant in San Francisco,* 1938, p. 62

The so-called Christian nations are the most enlightened and progressive . . . but in spite of their religion, not because of it. The Church has opposed every innovation and discovery from the day of Galileo down to our own time, when the use of anesthetics in childbirth was regarded as a sin because it avoided the biblical curse pronounced against Eve.

—Paine, *Mark Twain: A Biography,*
1912, vol. 3, p. 1534

During many ages there were witches. The Bible said so. The Bible commanded that they should not be allowed to live. Therefore the church . . . imprisoned, tortured, hanged, and burned whole hordes and armies of witches, and washed the Christian world clean with their foul blood. Then it was discovered that there was no such thing as witches, and never had been.

—"Bible Teaching and Religious
Practice," essay, 1923

Two or three centuries from now it will be recognized that all the competent killers are Christians; then the pagan world will go to school to the Christian—not to acquire his religion, but his guns.

—"The Mysterious Stranger," story,
1916, ch. 8

There are two kinds of Christian morals, one private and the other public. These two are so distinct, so unrelated, that they are no more akin to each other than are archangels and politicians.

—"Private and Public Morals,"
speech, 1906

The minister gave out his text and droned along monotonously through an argument that was so prosy that many a head by and by began to nod—and yet it was an argument that dealt in limitless fire and brimstone and thinned the predestined elect down to a company so small as to be hardly worth the saving.

—*Tom Sawyer,* 1876, ch. 5

CHURCH

The church is always trying to get other people to reform; it might not be a bad idea to reform itself a little by way of example.

—*A Tramp Abroad,* 1880, vol. 2, ch. 7

The Church . . . is credited with having spilt more innocent blood since the beginning of its supremacy, than all the political wars put together have spilt.

—DeVoto, *Letters from the Earth,* 1962,
Letter 11

There warn't anybody at the church, except maybe a hog or two, for there warn't any lock on the door, and hogs like a puncheon floor in summertime because it's cool. If you notice, most folks don't go to church only when they've got to; but a hog is different.

—*Huckleberry Finn,* 1884, ch. 18

There cannot be any excuse for our church-bells at home, for there is no family in America without a clock, and consequently there is no fair pretext for the usual Sunday medley of dreadful sounds that issues from our steeples.

—*A Tramp Abroad,* 1880, vol. 2, ch. 7

A man is accepted into a church for what he believes and he is turned out for what he knows.

—Attributed

CHURCHILL, WINSTON

Mark Twain met Winston Churchill at a London dinner in 1900, when Churchill was beginning to gain notoriety as a statesman. The two men left the party together and went outside for a smoke. Sir William Vernon Hartcourt remarked, as they departed, that whichever one of those two great talkers got the floor first would keep it, and he speculated that since Twain was an older and more experienced conversationalist, Churchill's voice would probably get its first good rest in years.

When the two men returned, Hartcourt asked Churchill whether he had enjoyed himself, and Churchill replied with much enthusiasm, "Yes!" Hartcourt turned to Twain and asked the same question.

Mark Twain paused, puffed his cigar and said, "I have had a good smoke."

He was now very old and snow-white [wrote Churchill of the meeting in *My Early Life,* 1930], and combined with a noble air a most delightful style of conversation. Of course we argued about the [Boer] war. After some interchanges I

40

found myself beaten back to the citadel "My country right or wrong." "Ah," said the old gentleman, "When the poor country is fighting for its life, I agree. But this was not your case." I think however that I did not displease him; for he was good enough at my request to sign every one of the thirty volumes of his works for my benefit; and in the first volume he inscribed the following maxim intended, I dare say, to convey a gentle admonition: "To do good is noble; to teach others to do good is nobler, and no trouble."

CIRCUMSTANCE

Circumstances make man, not man circumstances.

—Notebook, 1902

Circumstance furnished the capital, and my temperament told me what to do with it.

—"The Turning Point of My Life,"
essay, 1910

We are strange beings, we seem to go free, but we go in chains—chains of training, custom, convention, association, environment—in a word, Circumstance—and against these bonds the strongest of us struggle in vain.

—"3,000 Years Among the Microbes,"
story, 1905

CIVILIZATION

Civilization: A limitless multiplication of unnecessary necessaries.

—Attributed

Can we afford Civilization?

—"To the Person Sitting in
Darkness," essay, 1901

Is it, perhaps, possible that there are two kinds of Civilization—one for home consumption and one for the heathen market?

—"To the Person Sitting in
Darkness," essay, 1901

The peoples furthest from civilization are the ones where equality between man and woman are furthest apart. . . . No civilization can be perfect until exact equality between man and woman is included.

—Notebook, 1895

Is there no salvation for us but to adopt Civilization and lift ourselves down to its level?

—"To the Person Sitting in
Darkness," essay, 1901

Extending the Blessings of Civilization to our Brother who Sits in Darkness has been a good trade and has paid well, on the whole; and there is money in it yet, if carefully worked—but not enough, in my judgment, to make any considerable risk advisable.

—"To the Person Sitting in
Darkness," essay, 1901

There are many humorous things in the world; among them, the white man's notion that he is less savage than the other savages.

—*Following the Equator*, 1897, vol. 1, ch. 21

CIVIL WAR

Mark Twain, like the nation itself, was divided by the Civil War. He was opposed to slavery, but he was a Missourian too, and Missouri was on the Confederate side. Mark Twain served in the Confederate Army for two weeks, but his heart was never in it, and he decided to retire. "There was but one honorable course for me to pursue and I pursued it," he said. "I withdrew to private life and gave the Union cause a chance."

Twain withdrew from the Civil War and went west, where his literary career began. His decision to leave Missouri and go to Nevada had far-reaching consequences. "It was not my presence in the Civil War that determined that tremendous contest—it was my retirement from it that brought the crash. It left the Confederate side too weak."

CLASSIC

A classic is something that everybody wants to have read and nobody wants to read.

—"The Disappearance of Literature,"
speech, 1900

CLEVELAND, GROVER

Among the celebrities who sometimes spent their summers in Tyringham in Berkshire County, Massachusetts, were Mark Twain and Grover Cleveland. Cleveland, the twenty-second President of the United States, was a large, stout gentleman who, like Twain, enjoyed fishing.

One day someone observed that Mark Twain was not "wetting a line," and inquired the reason. Twain answered with a sigh, "Cleveland is using the pond."

CLOTHES

Returning from a trip to Europe, Mark Twain grew impatient as a customs official rummaged through his baggage.

"My good friend," said the author, as politely as he could, "you don't have to trouble yourself. There are only clothes in there—nothing but clothes."

But the suspicious official continued poking about until he struck something solid. He reached into the suitcase and pulled out a quart of the finest-quality bourbon.

"Just clothes, eh?" gloated the official. "You call this 'just clothes'? "

"Sure," replied Mark Twain calmly. "That is my nightcap."

Clothes make the man. Naked people have little or no influence in society.

—Johnson, *More Maxims of Mark,* 1927, p. 6

Modesty died when clothes were born.

—Paine, *Mark Twain: A Biography,* 1912,
vol. 3, p. 1514

Their costumes, as to architecture, were the latest fashion inten-sified; they were rainbow-hued; they were hung with jewels—chiefly diamonds. It would have been plain to any eye that it had cost something to upholster these women.

—*The Gilded Age*, 1873, ch. 33
(description of a fashionable party in
Washington, D.C.)

We must put up with our clothes as they are—they have their reason for existing. They are on us to expose us—to advertise what we wear them to conceal.

—*Following the Equator*, 1897, vol. 2, ch. 1

You have never seen a person with clothes on. Oh, well, you haven't lost anything.

—Satan to the archangels, in DeVoto,
Letters from the Earth, 1962, Letter 3

COCKTAILS

When Mark Twain returned to America in 1879 on the ocean liner *Gallia* after seventeen months abroad, he told reporters it was smooth sailing compared to the *Quaker City* of *Innocents Abroad* fame. He said the *Gallia* was so steady that if you stood a goblet loose on the shelf at night it would still be there in the morning. A reporter from the *New York Times* then asked if a cocktail left standing on the shelf would still be there in the morning.

Mark Twain replied, "The ship is hardly steady enough for that."

COFFEE

During a stay in Germany, Mark Twain found grounds for com-plaint about the poor quality of German coffee. His theory was that German coffee was prepared by "rubbing a chicory bean against a coffee bean and dropping the chicory bean in the water."

The best coffee in Europe, he claimed, was Vienna coffee, compared to which all other coffee "is mere fluid poverty."

Mark Twain had very strict standards for coffee. Once, when

he was served a cup of substandard variety, he commented, "It is inferior for coffee, but it is pretty fair tea."

COLD

Cold! If the thermometer had been an inch longer we'd all have frozen to death!

—Read, *Mark Twain and I,* 1940, p. 44

COMMUNISM

Communism is idiocy. They want to divide up the property. Suppose they did it—it requires brains to keep money as well as make it. In a precious little while the money would be back in the former owner's hands and the communist would be poor again.

—Notebook, 1879

COMPLIMENTS

"There is nothing you can say in answer to a compliment," said a blushing Mark Twain after a complimentary introduction to a crowd in Jamestown, Virginia. "I have been complimented myself a great many times, and they always embarrass me—I always feel they have not said enough."

I can live for two months on a good compliment.

—Paine, *Mark Twain: A Biography,*
1912, vol. 3, p. 1334

An author values a compliment even when it comes from a source of doubtful competency.

—Neider, *Autobiography,* 1959, ch. 50

An occasional compliment is necessary, to keep up one's self-respect. . . . When you cannot get a compliment any other way pay yourself one.

—Notebook, 1894

I tell you it is a talent by itself to pay compliments gracefully and have them ring true. It's an art by itself.

—"I Was Born for a Savage," speech, 1907

None but an ass pays a compliment and asks a favor at the same time. There are many asses.

—Notebook, 1902

CONFORMITY

The natural instinct to passively yield to that vague something recognized as authority . . .

—"Corn-pone Opinions," essay, 1923

It is our nature to conform; it is a force which not many can successfully resist. What is its seat? The inborn requirement of self-approval.

—"Corn-pone Opinions," essay, 1923

In morals, conduct, and beliefs we take the color of our environment and associations, and it is a color that can be safely warranted to wash.

—"Is Shakespeare Dead?" essay, 1909

CONGRESS

Suppose you were an idiot. And suppose you were a member of Congress. But I repeat myself.

—Paine, *Mark Twain: A Biography,* 1912, vol. 2, p. 724

Fleas can be taught nearly anything that a Congressman can.

—"What Is Man?" essay, 1906

Whiskey is carried into committee rooms in demijohns and carried out in demagogues.

—Notebook, 1868

CONSCIENCE

An uneasy conscience is a hair in the mouth.

—Notebook, 1904

I have noticed my conscience for many years, and I know it is more trouble and bother to me than anything else I started with.

—*A Connecticut Yankee*, 1889, ch. 18

It takes up more room than all the rest of a person's insides.

—*Huckleberry Finn*, 1884, ch. 34

If you grant that *one* man's conscience doesn't know right from wrong, it is an admission that there are others like it. This single admission pulls down the whole doctrine of infallibility of judgment in consciences.

—"What Is Man?" essay, 1906

Our consciences take *no* notice of pain inflicted on others until it reaches a point where it gives pain to *us*.

—"What Is Man?" essay, 1906

It seems to me that a man should secure the *well done, faithful servant,* of his own conscience *first* and foremost, and let all other loyalties go.

—"Consistency," speech, 1887

CONSENSUS

Do you know of a case where a Consensus won a game?

—"Dr. Loeb's Incredible Discovery," essay, 1923

CONSERVATIVE

The radical of one century is the conservative of the next. The radical invents the views. When he has worn them out the conservative adopts them.

—Notebook, 1898

CONSISTENCY

Who is the really consistent man? The man who changes. Since change is the natural law of his being, he cannot be consistent if he stick in a rut.

—"Consistency," speech, 1887

There are those who would misteach us that to stick in a rut is consistency—and a virtue; and that to climb out of the rut is inconsistency—and a vice.

—"Consistency," speech, 1887

In truth you are always consistent, always yourself, always an ass.

—"Carnival of Crime in Connecticut,"
story, 1876

CONVERSATION

Mark Twain once remarked to Norman Hapgood that people in the East tend to talk about money matters all the time. It was hard for a modest Midwesterner to get used to it.

"Now, in Hannibal, Missouri, where I was brought up, we never talked about money," said Twain. "There was not enough money in the place to furnish a topic of conversation."

CONVICTION

Whatever you say, say it with conviction.

—Clara Clemens, *My Father, Mark
Twain*, 1931, p. 134

COOPER, JAMES FENIMORE

Cooper's art has some defects. In one place in *Deerslayer,* and in the restricted space of two-thirds of a page, Cooper has scored 114 offenses against literary art out of a possible 115. It breaks the record.

—"Fenimore Cooper's Literary
Offenses," essay, 1895

COURAGE

Courage is resistance to fear, mastery of fear, not absence of fear.

—*Pudd'nhead Wilson*, 1894, ch. 12

Except a creature be part coward, it is not a compliment to say he is brave.

—*Pudd'nhead Wilson*, 1894, ch. 12

There are not enough morally brave men in stock. We are out of moral-courage material.

—"The United States of Lyncherdom,"
essay, 1923

COURTESY

What is courtesy? Consideration for others. Is there a good deal of it in the American character? So far as I have observed, no. Is it an American characteristic? So far as I have observed, the most prominent, the most American of all American characteristics, is the poverty of it in the American character.

—"Doctor Van Dyke," speech, 1906

COWARDICE

There are several good protections against temptations but the surest is cowardice.

—*Following the Equator*, 1897, vol. 1, ch. 36

We all live in the protection of certain cowardices which we call our principles.

—Johnson, *More Maxims of Mark*, 1927,
p. 14

The human race is a race of cowards; and I am not only marching in that procession but carrying a banner.

—DeVoto, *Mark Twain in Eruption*, 1940,
preface

CREATION

Where was the use, originally, in rushing this whole globe through in six days? It is likely that if more time had been taken, in the first place, the world would have been made right, and this ceaseless improving and repairing would not be necessary now.

—Life on the Mississippi, 1883, ch. 51

CREDIBILITY

As a young boy, Mark Twain showed some flashes of the story-telling gift that would one day entertain the world, especially when it was necessary for him to explain why he had missed school or failed to perform some duty.

He soon acquired a reputation in Hannibal for telling stories that were taller than he was. A neighbor once asked his mother, "Do you ever believe *anything* that boy says?"

Mrs. Clemens replied, "I know his average, therefore he never deceives me. I discount him 90 percent for embroidery, and what is left is perfect and priceless truth, without a flaw in it anywhere." She added: "He is a wellspring of truth, but you can't bring up the whole well with one bucket."

CRIME

By curious coincidence, it happened that whenever Mark Twain visited a foreign country a crime would occur there during his stay. He denied vehemently that this was anything but a coincidence, yet his denials sometimes created more doubts than they dispelled. When during a visit he made to England in 1907 the Ascot Cup was stolen, Mark Twain made this comment to the press: "People say it is a curious coincidence that the Ascot Cup and the regalia from Dublin Castle should have been stolen during my stay. And so it is."

Twain thought that would be the end of it, but it wasn't. It only seemed to invite more inquiries. In his speech "The Begum of Bengal," Twain defended himself: "It is rumor. Nobody comes out and charges me with carrying out that robbery. It is mere human testimony, and it does not amount to testimony, it is merely rumor, circumstantial evidence, mere human speech, assertion, rumor and suspicion. But circumstantial evidence is the best evidence in the world."

Not even this impassioned disavowal succeeded in silencing speculation on the subject, and before Twain left England he confessed to the crime.

So I simply declare in all my sincerity and with my hand on my heart that I never heard of that diamond robbery till I saw it in the morning paper. And I can say with perfect truth that I never saw that box of dynamite till the police came to inquire of me if I had any more of it.

—Speech during a visit to Canada,
1881

It could probably be shown by facts and figures that there is no distinctly native American criminal class except Congress.

—*Following the Equator*, 1897, vol. 1, ch. 8

They [the young pirates] inwardly resolved that so long as they remained in the business their piracies should not again be sullied with the crime of stealing.

—*Tom Sawyer*, 1876, ch. 13

It was without a compeer among swindles. It was perfect, it was rounded, symmetrical, complete, colossal!

—*Life on the Mississippi*, 1883, ch. 52

They put the beginners in with the confirmed criminals. This would be well if man were naturally inclined to good, but he isn't, and so *association* makes the beginners worse than they were when they went into captivity.

—"What Is Man?" essay, 1906 (on
the prison system)

As by the fires of experience, so by commission of crime you learn real morals. Commit all the crimes, familiarize yourself with all sins, take them in rotation (there are only two or three thousand of them), stick to it, commit two or three every day, and by and by you will be proof against them. When you are through you will be proof against all sins and morally perfect.

—"On Being Morally Perfect,"
speech, 1899

CRITICS

I like criticism, but it must be my way.

—Paine, *Autobiography*, 1924, vol. 2, p. 247

One mustn't criticize other people on grounds where he can't stand perpendicular himself.

—*A Connecticut Yankee*, 1889, ch. 26

It is easy to find fault, if one has that disposition. There was once a man who, not being able to find any other fault with his coal, complained that there were too many prehistoric toads in it.

—*Pudd'nhead Wilson*, 1894, ch. 9

I don't mind what the opposition say of me so long as they don't tell the truth about me. But when they descend to telling the truth about me I consider that this is taking an unfair advantage.

—Speech at a Republican rally, 1879

It is the will of God that we must have critics, and missionaries, and congressmen, and humorists, and we must bear the burden.

—Paine, *Autobiography*, 1924, vol. 2, p. 69

CUSTOM

There isn't anything you can't stand, if you are only born and bred to it.

—*A Connecticut Yankee*, 1889, ch. 8

Often, the less there is to justify a traditional custom the harder it is to get rid of it.

—*Tom Sawyer*, 1876, ch. 5

Laws are sand, customs are rock. Laws can be evaded and punishment escaped, but an openly transgressed custom brings sure punishment.

—"The Gorky Incident," essay, 1906

Customs do not concern themselves with right or wrong or reason.

—"The Gorky Incident," essay, 1906

Custom is a petrifaction; nothing but dynamite can dislodge it for a century.

—"Diplomatic Pay and Clothes,"
essay, 1899

A crime persevered in a thousand centuries ceases to be a crime, and becomes a virtue. This is the law of custom, and custom supersedes all other forms of law.

—*Following the Equator*, 1897, vol. 2, ch. 27

DANCING

I had longed to be a butterfly, and I was one at last. I attended private parties in sumptuous evening dress, simpered and aired my graces like a born beau, and polkaed and schotisched with a step peculiar to myself—and the kangaroo.

—*Roughing It*, 1872, ch. 58
(after he finally found employment in
San Francisco)

DEATH

In his later years, Mark Twain was haunted by rumors of his death. The rumors began while he was living reclusively in London after the death of his daughter Susy from meningitis in 1896. It was a sad time for Mark Twain, and he stayed out of sight. In America, there were rumors he was ill.

When a distant relative of Samuel Clemens, Dr. James Clemens, moved to London from St. Louis in 1897, a St. Louis newspaper asked the doctor to find his famous cousin and see if he was all right. Dr. Clemens reported back that Samuel Clemens was living quietly, but was not ill. Confusion mushroomed when James Clemens himself fell ill. Other newspapers soon had it that Samuel Clemens was on the brink of death.

Finally, a young reporter located Mark Twain in London. The reporter was carrying cabled instructions from his paper, which he reluctantly exhibited on request:

"If Mark Twain very ill, five hundred words. If dead, send one thousand."

When Mark Twain saw those instructions, he smiled grimly and made his famous reply: "Just say the report of my death has been greatly exaggerated."

The next day that line was heard around the world. Ironically, Twain had the opportunity to repeat the line on numerous occasions, for there were recurring rumors of his death. And these rumors have persisted even to the present day, when, despite repeated denials and much evidence to the contrary, there are many people who believe those false reports of Mark Twain's death.

The reports of my death are greatly exaggerated.

Cablegram, 1897 and thereafter

There is no such thing as death.

—"3,000 Years Among the Microbes,"
story, 1905

All say, "How hard it is that we have to die"—a strange complaint to come from the mouths of people who have had to live.

—*Pudd'nhead Wilson,* 1894, ch. 10

Pity is for the living, envy is for the dead.

—*Following the Equator,* 1897, vol. 1, ch. 19

Death, the refuge, the solace, the best and kindliest and most prized friend and benefactor of the erring, the forsaken, the old and weary and broken of heart . . .

—"Adam," speech, 1880s

People ought to start dead and then they would be honest so much earlier.

—Neider, *Autobiography*, 1959, ch. 55

I think we never become really and genuinely our entire and honest selves until we are dead—and not then until we have been dead years and years.

—Neider, *Autobiography*, 1959, ch. 55

Well, it is best to have a supply of memorials to guard against accidents. I mean to have an assortment of tombstones myself.

—"An English Notebook," in DeVoto,
Letters from the Earth, 1962

DEATHBED REMARKS

A writer has two chances for last words. Mark Twain's last written statement was a memorandum on the subject of death:

"Death, the only immortal who treats us all alike, whose pity and whose peace and whose refuge are for all—the soiled and the pure, the rich and the poor, the loved and the unloved."

Mark Twain prepared this eloquent memorandum a few days ahead of time, so the press would have some last words to quote. He did not want to go out on a flat note. "I do wish our great men would quit saying these flat things just at the moment they die," he had written years before in an essay on famous last words.

There is some question about Mark Twain's last actual spoken words, but according to his attending physician, Dr. Edward Quintard, who was standing by the bed, Mark Twain whispered an unfinished thought: "If we meet . . ."

DECEPTION

When a person cannot deceive himself the chances are against his being able to deceive other people.

—Neider, *Autobiography,* 1959, ch. 36

DEDICATION

Mark Twain dedicated his first published book, *The Celebrated Jumping Frog of Calaveras County and Other Sketches* (1867) to the infamous John Smith:

"To John Smith, whom I have known in diverse and sundry places about the world, and whose many and manifold virtues did always command my esteem, I dedicate this book."

He had a wily reason for dedicating the book to John Smith. This explanation appeared just below the dedication:

"It is said that a man to whom a book is dedicated always buys a copy. If this is true in this instance, a princely affluence is about to descend on the author."

DEMOCRACY

Strip the human race absolutely naked and it would be a real democracy.

—Notebook, 1897

We adore titles and heredities in our hearts and ridicule them with our mouths. This is our democratic privilege.

—Neider, *Autobiography,* 1959, ch. 34

Where every man in a state has a vote, brutal laws are impossible.

—*A Connecticut Yankee,* 1889, ch. 25

DENTISTRY

When Mark Twain was a boy, dental care was even more traumatic than today. "When teeth became touched with decay or were otherwise ailing, the doctor knew but one thing to do—he fetched his tongs and dragged them out," recalled Twain. "If the jaw remained, it was not his fault."

But worst, most cursed of all, were the dentists who made too many parenthetical remarks—"dentists who secure your instant and breathless interest in a tooth by taking a grip on it, and then stand there and drawl through a tedious anecdote before they give the dreaded jerk. Parentheses in literature and dentistry are in bad taste."

DESCRIPTION

In applying for a German passport on May 7, 1878, Mark Twain described himself to the authorities. "My description is as follows: Born 1835; 5 ft. 8½ inches tall; weight about 145 pounds . . . dark brown hair and red moustache, full face with very high ears and light gray beautiful beaming eyes and a damned good moral character."

DESIRE

A great law of human action—in order to make a man or a boy covet a thing, it is only necessary to make the thing difficult to attain.

—*Tom Sawyer*, 1876, ch. 2

A human being has a natural desire to have more of a good thing than he needs.

—*Following the Equator*, 1897, vol. 1, ch. 14

DICTIONARY

Mark Twain, the honored guest at a grammar school graduation, was presenting awards to the students. One little boy's prize was a big Webster's dictionary. "This is a very interesting and useful book, my son," said Twain, bestowing it upon him. "I have studied it often, but I never could discover the plot."

DIET

A budding young author, who lacked nothing but talent, once wrote to Mark Twain inquiring what was the ideal diet for a writer. He wanted to know if it was true, as Professor Agassiz of Harvard had said, that fish was good brain food.

Mark Twain wrote in reply: "Yes, Agassiz does recommend authors to eat fish, because the phosphorus in it makes brain. So far you are correct. But I cannot help you to a decision about the amount you need to eat—at least, not with certainty. If the specimen composition you send is about your fair usual average, I should judge that perhaps a *couple of whales* would be all you would want for the present."

In the matter of diet—I have been persistently strict in sticking to the things which didn't agree with me until one or the other of us got the best of it.

—Seventieth-birthday speech, 1905

DIFFERENCES

It were not best that we should all think alike; it is difference of opinion that makes horse races.

—*Pudd'nhead Wilson,* 1894, ch. 19

People are different. And it is the best way.

—"Tom Sawyer, Detective," story, 1894, ch. 2

DIPLOMATS

They want to send me abroad, as a Consul or a Minister. I said I didn't want any of the pie. God knows I am mean enough and lazy enough, now, without being a foreign consul.

—Letter to Jane Clemens, February 6, 1868

DISAPPOINTMENT

One cannot have everything the way he would like it. A man has no business to be depressed by a disappointment, anyway; he ought to make up his mind to get even.

—*A Connecticut Yankee,* 1889, ch. 22

DISARMAMENT

In 1899, when European disarmament was proposed, William T. Stead, the editor of the *Review of Reviews,* wrote to Mark Twain asking his opinion on the issue. Twain wrote back, saying that he was ready to disarm. This is the entire letter:

> Dear Mr. Stead: The Tsar is ready to disarm. I am ready to disarm. Collect the others; it should not be much of a task now.
>
> Mark Twain

DISCOVERY

What is it that confers the noblest delight? What is that which swells a man's breast with pride above that which any other experience can bring to him? Discovery! To know that you are walking where none others have walked; that you are beholding what human eye has not seen before; that you are breathing a virgin atmosphere. To give birth to an idea—to discover a great thought.

—Innocents Abroad, 1869, ch. 26

DOCTORS

Mark Twain testified before a legislative committee in Albany, New York, on February 27, 1901, in support of a bill to legalize osteopathy. He told the committee this story:

> At a time during my younger days my attention was attracted to a picture of a house which bore the inscription, "Christ Disputing with the Doctors." I could attach no other meaning to it than that Christ was actually quarrelling with the doctors. So I asked an old slave, who was a sort of a herb doctor in a small way—unlicensed, of course—what the meaning of the picture was. "What has he done?" I asked.
>
> And the colored man replied: "Humph, he ain't got no license."

DOGS

"I remember when I had just written *Innocents Abroad,*" recalled Mark Twain at an Associated Press banquet, "when I and my partner wanted to start a newspaper syndicate. We needed three dollars and did not know where to get it. While we were in a quandary, I espied a valuable dog on the street. I picked up the canine and sold him to a man for three dollars. Afterward the owner of the dog came along and I got three dollars from him for telling where the dog was. So I went back and gave the three dollars to the man whom I sold it to, and lived honestly for ever after."

If you pick up a starving dog and make him prosperous, he will not bite you. This is the principal difference between a dog and a man.

—*Pudd'nhead Wilson,* 1894, ch. 16

Heaven goes by favor. If it went by merit, you would stay out and your dog would go in.

—Paine, *Mark Twain: A Biography,*
1912, vol. 3, p. 1567

DOLLAR

Mark Twain was reported to earn a dollar a word for his writing. Alluding to this, a prankster once enclosed a dollar bill with a note to Mark Twain, saying, "Please send me a word."

A prompt reply arrived from Mark Twain. It contained one word: "Thanks."

DOOR

Shut the door. Not that it lets in the cold but that it lets out the coziness.

—Notebook, 1898

DOUBLES

Mark Twain frequently received photographs of men who supposedly looked like him. Eventually he grew weary of the "Mark Twain look-alike" correspondence and so he asked his printer to run off a few hundred copies of the following form letter:

> My dear Sir: I thank you very much for your letter and your photograph. In my opinion you are more like me than any other of my numerous doubles. I may even say that you resemble me more closely than I do myself. In fact, I intend to use your picture to shave by.
>
> > Yours thankfully,
> > S. Clemens

DREAMS

The castle-building habit, the day-dreaming habit—how it grows! . . . and how soon and how easily our dream life and our material life become so intermingled and so fused together that we can't quite tell which is which, any more.

—"The $30,000 Bequest," story, 1904

In our dreams—I know it!—we do make the journeys we seem to make; we do see the things we seem to see; the people, the horses, the cats . . . are real, not chimeras; they are living spirits, not shadows; and they are immortal and indestructible.

—"My Platonic Sweetheart," story, 1916

DRESS

Mark Twain placed a higher value on comfort than appearance, and was inclined to call on friends and neighbors without wearing a tie or a collar. His wife, a good Victorian woman, upbraided him for this fault more than once. One day she caught him returning from a visit to their neighbor Harriet Beecher Stowe—the author of *Uncle Tom's Cabin*—tieless and collarless. Mrs. Clemens scolded him severely.

Twain went upstairs, extracted a tie and a collar from his closet, wrapped the items up in a box, and sent the box to his neighbor's house with this note attached:

"Herewith receive a call from the rest of me."

Mrs. Stowe sent back a note saying that she believed Mark Twain had discovered a new principle, that of making calls by installments. "I wonder," she wrote, "whether in extreme cases a man might not send his hat, coat, and boots, and be otherwise excused?"

I would rather go to bed with Lillian Russell stark naked than Ulysses S. Grant in full military regalia.

—Attributed

Some civilized women would lose half their charm without dress and some would lose all of it.

—"Woman, God Bless Her!" speech, 1882

DRINKING

When Bill Nye was appointed governor of the Nevada Territory, he went to Carson City to assume his official duties, and Mark Twain accompanied him.

The boys in Carson City decided to put the Easterner and his friend in their places by throwing them a big banquet and drinking them under the table, according to the Western custom. The night of the banquet the drinks flowed freely, hour after hour, and one by one the wobbly men sank to the floor and slumbered beneath the tablecloths.

Finally, in the wee hours of the morning, there were only two men left in an upright position—the two guests of honor, Bill Nye and Mark Twain.

Twain surveyed the sleepy scene and stood up from his chair. "Bill, let's get out of here," he said, "and go somewhere and get a drink."

Scotch whisky . . . I always take it at night as a preventive of toothache. I have never had the toothache; and what is more, I never intend to have it.

—"Letters to Satan," *Europe and Elsewhere,* 1923

I didn't regard it as a vice, because he was a Scotchman, and Scotch whisky to a Scotchman is as innocent as milk to the rest of the human race.

—Neider, *Autobiography,* 1959, ch. 30

What marriage is to morality, a properly conducted licensed liquor traffic is to sobriety.

—Notebook, 1895

DUELS

Much as the modern French duel is ridiculed by certain smart people, it is in reality one of the most dangerous institutions of our day. Since it is always fought in the open air the combatants are nearly sure to catch cold.

—*A Tramp Abroad,* 1880, vol. 1, ch. 3

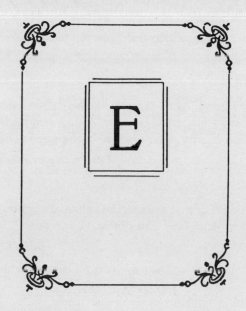

ECCENTRIC

Mark Twain ran into a friend one day at the races in England. Both men had been unlucky with their bets.

"I think the horse is more intelligent than man," said Mark Twain in disgust. "Have you ever heard of a horse going broke betting on a man?"

"Mark, I hate to have to ask you this," said his friend, sheepishly, "but can you buy me a ticket back to London?"

"Well, I'm nearly broke myself," confessed Twain. "But I'll tell you what I'll do. You can hide under my seat and I'll conceal you with my legs." The friend agreed to go along with this scheme.

Twain then went to the ticket counter and bought two tickets. As the train pulled out of the station, his friend was crouching under the seat. After a few minutes, the conductor came around collecting tickets and Twain handed him two. "But where is the other passenger?" inquired the perplexed conductor.

"Oh, that's my friend's ticket!" Mark Twain replied in a loud voice. "He is a bit eccentric and likes to ride under the seat!"

EDITORS

How often we recall, with regret, that Napoleon once shot at a magazine editor and missed him and killed a publisher. But we remember with charity, that his intentions were good.

—Letter to Henry Alden, November 11, 1906

I am not the editor of a newspaper, and shall always try to do right and be good, so that God will not make me one.

—*Galaxy Magazine*, 1870

EDUCATION

The formal schooling of Samuel Clemens ended at the age of twelve when he was apprenticed to a printer in Hannibal. The education of Mark Twain continued, however, in riverboat cabins and silver mines and lecture halls and publishers' offices, everywhere he went, for the rest of his life. He said, "I never let my schooling interfere with my education."

Soap and education are not as sudden as a massacre, but they are more deadly in the long run.

—"Facts Concerning the Recent Resignation," sketch, 1867

It is noble to teach oneself, but still nobler to teach others—and less trouble.

—"Doctor Van Dyke," speech, 1906

The self-taught man seldom knows anything accurately, and he does not know a tenth as much as he could have known if he had worked under teachers, and besides, he brags, and is the means of fooling other thoughtless people into going and doing as he himself has done.

—"Taming the Bicycle," essay, 1917

It is better to support schools than jails.

—"Feeding a Dog on Its Own Tail,"
speech, 1900

Out of the public school grows the greatness of a nation.

—"Feeding a Dog on Its Own Tail,"
speech, 1900

All schools, all colleges, have two great functions: to confer, and to conceal valuable knowledge.

—Notebook, 1908

Apparently—like our public-school boy—his "education" consists in learning *things,* not the meaning of them; he is fed upon the husks, not the corn.

—*Following the Equator,* 1897, vol. 2, ch. 25

Everything has its limit—iron ore cannot be educated into gold.

—"What Is Man?" essay, 1906

Education consists mainly in what we have unlearned.

—Notebook, 1898

In the first place God made idiots. This was for practice. Then He made school boards.

—*Following the Equator,* 1897, vol. 2, ch. 25

ELIOT, GEORGE

I bored through *Middlemarch* the past week . . . and nearly died from the overwork.

—Letter to William Dean Howells, 1885

EMBARRASSMENT

In 1868, when Mark Twain was working as a newspaper correspondent in Washington, D.C., he was introduced to Ulysses S. Grant, who would be President within a year. As Mark Twain, who was not yet famous, looked into Grant's stony, unsmiling face, he found himself, for the first time in his life, with absolutely nothing to say.

After an awkward silence, Twain finally summoned the courage to speak. "General, I seem to be slightly embarrassed," he said. "Are you?" The severe general cracked up.

Eleven years later, after Mark Twain delivered his "Babies" speech at a banquet in Grant's honor, the two men met again. Grant came up to Twain and shook his hand. "Mr. Clemens, I am not embarrassed," he said, grinning. "Are you?"

Mark Twain was flattered that Grant still remembered their first meeting after so many years. But he was not surprised. "He would remember me, because I was the person who did not ask him for an office."

EMOTIONS

Emotions are among the toughest things in the world to manufacture out of whole cloth; it is easier to manufacture seven facts than one emotion.

—*Life on the Mississippi,* 1883, ch. 27

All emotion is involuntary when genuine.

—"Cooper's Prose Style," essay, in DeVoto, *Letters from the Earth,* 1962

ENERGY

What is government without energy? And what is a man without energy? Nothing—nothing at all. What is the grandest thing in Paradise Lost—the Arch Fiend's terrible energy! What was the greatest feature in Napoleon's character? His unconquerable energy! Sum all the gifts that man is endowed with, and we give our greatest share of admiration to his energy. And today, if I were a heathen, I would rear a statue to Energy, and fall down and worship it!

—Paine, *Mark Twain: A Biography,*
1912, vol. 1, p. 146

ENGLISH

Mark Twain enjoyed teasing the English about their English. "When I speak my native tongue in its utmost purity in England," he said, "an Englishman can't understand me at all." He further commented on the barrier of our common language: "Some of the commonest English words are not in use with us—such as 'ousemaid, 'ospital, 'otel, 'istorian."

Mark Twain also liked to tease the English about their dimwittedness. After returning from a trip to England, Twain was asked by a Baltimore reporter about the English reputation for being reluctant to laugh.

The English are not less likely to laugh, Twain answered, but they are *slower* to laugh. "You talk to four or five Englishmen and tell them a funny story. When you get through they'll never smile," said Twain. "But next day they'll laugh."

The English are mentioned in the Bible; Blessed are the meek, for they shall inherit the earth

—*Following the Equator,* 1897, vol. 1, ch. 17

ENVY

Envy . . . the only thing which men will sell both body and soul to get.

—"Concerning the Jews," essay, 1899

Man will do many things to get himself loved, he will do all things to get himself envied.

—*Following the Equator,* 1879, vol. 1, ch. 21

EVE

The Garden is lost, but I have found *him,* and am content.

—Eve, in "Eve's Diary," story, 1905

I am the first wife; and in the last wife I shall be repeated.

—Eve, in "Eve's Diary," story, 1905

I was greatly interested in the incident of Eve and the serpent, and thought Eve's calmness was perfectly noble. I asked Mr. B. if he had ever heard of another woman who, being approached by a serpent, would not excuse herself and break for the nearest timber.

—"Is Shakespeare Dead?" essay, 1909

EVIL

Everyone is a moon, and has a dark side which he never shows to anybody.

—*Following the Equator,* 1897, vol. 2, ch. 30

EVOLUTION

It obliges me to renounce my allegiance to the Darwinian theory of the Ascent of Man from the Lower Animals; since it now seems plain to me that that theory ought to be vacated in favor of a new and truer one . . . the *Descent* of Man from the Higher Animals.

—"The Lowest Animal," essay, 1897

EXAGGERATION

In my enthusiasm I may have exaggerated the details a little but you will easily forgive me that fault since I believe it is the first time I have ever deflected from perpendicular fact.

—"Whittier's Birthday," speech, 1877

It is human to exaggerate the merits of the dead.

—Notebook, 1896

EXAMPLE

Few things are harder to put up with than the annoyance of a good example.

—*Pudd'nhead Wilson,* 1894, ch. 19

EXCUSES

A good storyteller usually has a good excuse. When Mark Twain arrived forty-five minutes late for a lecture in Burlington, Iowa, his excuse was eminently believable. He told the audience that his train from St. Louis had been delayed for repairs. "On the way they broke something. A dispute arose as to what it was that was broken. It took forty minutes to decide the dispute, and five minutes to repair the damage."

The girl who was rebuked for having borne an illegitimate child, excused herself by saying, "But it is such a *little* one."

—"To My Missionary Critics," essay,
1901

EXERCISE

I have never taken any exercise, except sleeping and resting, and I never intend to take any.

—Seventieth-birthday speech, 1905

EXPECTATIONS

When Major Edward Bowes, an old friend of Twain's from the West, first came to New York, a dinner was held in his honor, and Mark Twain attended it. As the dinner progressed, Major Bowes became pale and panicky.

"Don't you feel well?" inquired Mark Twain. "You look whiter than a fish-belly."

"I'm scared to death," said the Major. "I know I shall be called upon to speak and I'm sure I shan't be able to rise from my chair. When I stand up, my mind sits down!"

"Eddie," said Twain, "it may help you if you keep one thing in mind—just remember they don't expect much."

Bowes remembered those words and was never self-conscious about speaking in public again.

EXPERIENCE

War talk by men who have been in a war is always interesting; whereas moon talk by a poet who has not been in the moon is likely to be dull.

—*Life on the Mississippi*, 1883, ch. 45

Experience is an author's most valuable asset; experience is the thing that puts the muscle and the breath and the warm blood into the book he writes.

—"Is Shakespeare Dead?" essay, 1909

Experience, the only logic sure to convince a diseased imagination and restore it to rugged health.

—*The American Claimant*, 1892, ch. 23

We should be careful to get out of an experience only the wisdom that is in it—and stop there; lest we be like the cat that sits down on a hot stove-lid. She will never sit down on a hot stove-lid again—and that is well; but also she will never sit down on a cold one anymore.

—*Following the Equator*, 1897, vol. 1, ch. 11

FACTS

Get your facts first, and then you can distort them as much as you please.

—Quoted in Kipling, *Sea to Shining Sea*,
1899, Letter 37

The mere knowledge of a fact is pale; but when you come to *realize* your fact, it takes on color. It is all the difference between hearing of a man being stabbed to the heart, and seeing it done.

—*A Connecticut Yankee,* 1889, ch. 6

We do not deal much in facts when we are contemplating ourselves.

—"Does the Race of Man Love a
Lord?" essay, 1902

You get a leetle too much costumery onto your statements: Always dress a fact in tights, never in an ulster.

—*Life on the Mississippi,* 1883, ch. 34
(an ulster is a long, loose, heavy
overcoat)

FAITH

There are those who scoff at the school-boy, calling him frivolous and shallow. Yet it was the school-boy who said, "Faith is believing what you know ain't so."

—*Following the Equator,* 1897, vol. 1, ch. 12

FAME

Samuel Clemens's pen name became so well known that letters sent to Mark Twain without any address would reach him. One time, a few friends in New York, remembering the author's birthday, decided to send him a birthday card. They knew he was abroad but they did not know where, so they addressed it "Mark Twain, God Knows Where." A few weeks later, they received a terse telegram from Italy with only two words in it: "He did."

Another letter, addressed "The Devil Knows Where," also reached Mark Twain, eliciting this response: "*He* did, too."

By common consent of all the nations and all the ages the most valuable thing in this world is the homage of men, whether deserved or undeserved.

—"At the Shrine of St. Wagner,"
essay, 1891

If it can be proved that my fame reaches to Neptune and Saturn that will satisfy me.

—"I Was Born for a Savage," speech,
1907

To arrive at a just estimate of a renowned man's character one must judge it by the standards of his time, not ours.

—*Joan of Arc,* 1896, preface

FASHION

The most fashionably dressed lady was Mrs. G. C. She wore a pink satin dress, plain in front but with a good deal of rake to it—to the train, I mean; it was said to be two or three yards long. One could see it creeping along the floor some little time after the woman was gone.

—"A Fashion Item," *Sketches New and Old*, 1875

No woman can look as well out of fashion as in it.

—Walker, *Mark Twain's Travels with Mr. Brown*, 1940, p. 142

FATHER

It is a wise child that knows its own father, and an unusual one that unreservedly approves of him.

—Johnson, *More Maxims of Mark*, 1927, p. 9

When I was a boy of fourteen, my father was so ignorant I could hardly stand to have the old man around. But when I got to be twenty-one, I was astonished at how much he had learned in seven years.

—*Reader's Digest*, September 1937

FAT MAN

Mark Twain was in San Francisco in 1865 during a mild earthquake and he wrote an account of it for a Nevada newspaper. Dismissing the exaggerated reports of widespread devastation, Twain told how a fat man named Pete Hopkins, who weighed four hundred and thirty pounds, was shaken off Telegraph Hill, tumbled down the slope and landed on a three-story brick house. "The local papers, always misrepresenting things, ascribed the destruction of the house to the earthquake."

FEAR

I went right out the window. I took the sash with me. I didn't need the sash. But it seemed easier to take it than leave it behind.

—"Memories," speech, 1906
(on discovering a dead body in his
father's office at night)

Each man is afraid of his neighbor's disapproval—a thing which, to the general run of the human race, is more dreaded than wolves and death.

—"The United States of
Lyncherdom," essay, 1923

FEELINGS

We all do no end of feeling, and we mistake it for thinking.

—"Corn-pone Opinions," essay, 1923

But that is the way we are made: we don't reason, where we feel, we just feel.

—*A Connecticut Yankee,* 1889, ch. 11

I have a badgered, harassed feeling, a good part of my time.

—Letter to Jane Clemens, February
17, 1878

FISHING

Returning home after a weekend in the Maine woods, Mark Twain was lounging in the smoking car of the train to Boston. He could not resist the temptation to boast to the rustic-looking New Englander seated beside him about the twelve big fish he had caught.

"The season is closed for fishing now," he confided, "but just between you and me, my friend, out there in the baggage car I've got two hundred pounds of the best rock bass that you ever laid eyes on."

"Waal," drawled the New Englander, "that's interestin', but d'ye know who I am?"

"No," said Twain. "Who are you?"

"Waal," said the homespun gentleman, "I'm the state game warden."

Mark Twain puffed on his cigar. "That's interestin'," he said. "But d'ye know who I am?"

"No. Who are you?" asked the warden.

"I'm the damnedest liar in the United States!"

FLATTERY

A little white-haired old lady approached Mark Twain after a lecture one night and told him how much she had enjoyed his talk.

"I wanted to thank you personally," she explained, "because you said you *loved* old ladies."

"I do love old ladies," said Mark Twain. "And I also like them *your* age."

FLIES

Mark Twain was impressed by the durability of the flies that inhabited Mono Lake, California, high in the Sierra Nevada mountains. In *Roughing It,* he observed: "You can hold them under water as long as you please they do not mind it they are only proud of it. When you let them go, they pop up to the surface as dry as patent-office report."

The water at Mono Lake was of dubious drinkability, however, which may explain the flies' reluctance to drown in it. "A white man cannot drink the water of Mono Lake, for it is nearly pure lye," wrote Twain. "It is said that the Indians in the vicinity drink it sometimes, though. It is not improbable, for they are among the purest liars I ever saw. (There will be no additional charge for this joke, except to parties requiring an explanation of it. This joke has received high commendations from some of the ablest minds of the age.)"

Nothing is made in vain, but the fly came near it.

—Johnson, *More Maxims of Mark,* 1927,
p. 10

FOOD

Last spring I stopped frolicking with mince pie after midnight. Up to then I had always believed it wasn't loaded.

—Seventieth-birthday speech, 1905

On the continent, you can't get a rare beefsteak—everything is as overdone as a martyr.

Notebook, 1897

A man accustomed to American food and American domestic cookery would not starve to death suddenly in Europe; but I think he would gradually waste away, and eventually die.

—*A Tramp Abroad*, 1880, vol. 2, ch. 20

Ours was a reasonably comfortable ship, with the customary seagoing fare—plenty of good food furnished by the Deity and cooked by the Devil.

—*Following the Equator*, 1897, vol. 1, ch. 1

I thought tamarinds were made to eat, but that was probably not the idea. I ate several, and it seemed to me that they were rather sour that year. They pursed up my lips, till they resembled the stem end of a tomato, and I had to take my sustenance through a quill for twenty-four hours. . . . Only strangers eat tamarinds— but they only eat them once.

—*Roughing It*, 1872, ch. 63

Sagebrush is a very fair fuel, but as a vegetable it is a distinguished failure. Nothing can abide the taste of it but the jackass and his illegitimate child the mule.

—*Roughing It*, 1872, ch. 3

But when the time comes that man has had his dinner, then the true man comes to the surface.

—"Progress in Medicine," speech, 1902

FOOLS

Let us be thankful for the fools. But for them the rest of us could not succeed.

—*Following the Equator,* 1897, vol. 1, ch. 28

If you send a damned fool to St. Louis, and you don't tell them he's a damned fool, *they'll* never find out.

—*Life on the Mississippi,* 1883, ch. 53

Hain't we got all the fools in town on our side? And hain't that a big enough majority in any town?

—*Huckleberry Finn,* 1884, ch. 26

If all the fools in this world should die, lordly God how lonely I should be.

—Letter to his wife, Olivia, 1885

FORBIDDEN

The more things are forbidden, the more popular they become.

—*Notebook,* 1895

FOREIGNERS

They spell it Vinci and pronounce it Vinchy; foreigners always spell better than they pronounce.

—*Innocents Abroad,* 1869, ch. 19

FORGETFULNESS

One evening while delivering a speech, Mark Twain forgot a word, strained his memory, faltered, then fumed at his own forgetfulness:

"I'll forget the Lord's middle name sometime, right in the midst of a storm, when I need all the help I can get!"

FORTUNETELLERS

In 1895, when Mark Twain was bankrupt and $94,000 in debt because of the failure of his publishing firm, Charles Webster & Co., he went to see Madam Cheiro, a well-known palm reader. She predicted that in his sixty-eighth year—which would be 1903—he would become suddenly rich.

"I am superstitious," said Twain. "I kept the prediction in mind and often thought of it. When at last it came true, October 22, 1903, there was but a month and nine days to spare."

On that day, Mark Twain signed a contract with Harper's publishing company, giving them the rights to all his books. The contract made Mark Twain a wealthy man just in time to fulfill Madam Cheiro's prophecy, and it freed him from financial worries for the last seven years of his life.

FOURTH OF JULY

July 4. Statistics show that we lose more fools on this day than in all the other days of the year put together. This proves, by the number left in stock, that one Fourth of July per year is now inadequate, the country has grown so.

—*Pudd'nhead Wilson,* 1894, ch. 17

FREEDOM

Other places do seem so cramped up and smothery, but a raft don't. You feel mighty free and easy and comfortable on a raft.

—*Huckleberry Finn,* 1884, ch. 18

No people in the world ever did achieve their freedom by goody-goody talk and moral suasion: it being immutable law that all revolutions that will succeed, must begin in blood, whatever may answer afterward. If history teaches anything, it teaches that.

—*A Connecticut Yankee,* 1889, ch. 20

Loyalty to petrified opinions never yet broke a chain or freed a human soul.

—"Consistency," essay, 1923

FRENCH

In Paris they just simply opened their eyes and stared when we spoke to them in French! We never did succeed in making those idiots understand their own language.

—*Innocents Abroad*, 1869, ch. 61

When using that language I have often noticed that I have hardly ever been mistaken for a Frenchman, except perhaps by horses.

—"Visit to Canada," speech, 1881

In Paris . . . the law says, in effect, "It is the business of the weak to get out of the way of the strong." We fine a cabman if he runs over a citizen; Paris fines the citizen for being run over.

—*A Tramp Abroad*, 1880, vol. 2, ch. 18

French morality is not of that straight-laced description which is shocked at trifles.

—*Innocents Abroad*, 1869, ch. 14

The objects of which Paris folks are fond—literature, art, medicine and adultery.

—"The Corpse," speech, 1879

A joke in Chicago, you know, is a riddle in Paris.

—Fisher, *Abroad with Mark Twain*, 1922, p. 92

FREUD, SIGMUND

Sigmund Freud, the founder of psychoanalysis, wrote a book on humor, *Jokes and Their Relation to the Unconscious* (1905), in which he dissected some of Mark Twain's jokes. According to Freud's analysis, an "economy of pity" was the key to Twainian humor:

"An economy of pity is one of the most frequent sources of humorous pleasure. Mark Twain's humor usually works with this mechanism. In an account of his brother's life he tells us how he was at one time employed on a great roadmaking enterprise. The premature explosion of a mine blew him up into the air and he came down again far away from the place where he had been working. We are bound to have feelings of sympathy for the victim of the accident and would like to ask whether he was injured by it. But when the story goes on to say that his brother had a half-day's wages deducted for being 'absent from his place of employment' we are entirely distracted from our pity and become almost as hard-hearted as the contractor and almost as indifferent to possible damage to the brother's health."

FRIENDS

In November 1902, Colonel George Harvey, the president of Harper & Brothers, Mark Twain's publisher, gave a dinner in honor of the author's sixty-seventh birthday at the Metropolitan Club in New York. It was attended by many VIPs. During his speech that night, Mark Twain observed:

"I see around me captains of all the illustrious industries, most distinguished men. There are more than fifty here, and I believe I know thirty-nine of them well. I could probably borrow money from—from the others, anyway."

The holy passion of Friendship is of so sweet and steady and loyal and enduring a nature that it will last through a whole lifetime, if not asked to lend money.

—*Pudd'nhead Wilson*, 1894, ch. 8

It takes your enemy and your friend, working together, to hurt you to the heart; the one to slander you and the other to get the news to you.

—*Following the Equator*, 1897, vol. 2, ch. 9

The proper office of a friend is to side with you when you are in the wrong. Nearly anybody will side with you when you are in the right.

—Notebook, 1898

FRIVOLITY

Whenever I am rested and feeling good I can't help being frivolous.

—"The Begum of Bengal," speech,
1907

FUN

A good and wholesome thing is a little harmless fun in this world; it tones a body up and keeps him human and prevents him from souring.

—*Joan of Arc,* 1896, bk. 2, ch. 21

FUNERALS

When a blood relative sobs, an intimate friend should choke up, a distant acquaintance should sigh, a stranger should merely fumble sympathetically with his handkerchief.

—"Burlesque of Books of Etiquette,"
Letters from the Earth, 1962
(recommended etiquette at a funeral)

In order to know a community, one must observe the style of its funerals and know what manner of men they bury with most ceremony.

—*Roughing It,* 1872, ch. 47

GENIUS

Thousands of geniuses live and die undiscovered—either by themselves or by others.

—Neider, *Autobiography,* 1959, ch. 27

It is impossible that a genius—at least a literary genius—can ever be discovered by his intimates; they are so close to him that he is out of focus to them.

—Neider, *Autobiography,* 1959, ch. 27

Genius has no youth, but starts with the ripeness of age and old experience.

—Paine, *Mark Twain: A Biography,*
1912, vol. 2, p. 1089

GENTLEMAN

If any man has just, merciful and kindly instincts he would be a gentleman, for he would need nothing else in the world.

—"The Gentleman," speech, 1906
(responding to a request for a
definition)

He was a gentleman all over; and so was his family. He was well born, as the saying is, and that's worth as much in a man as it is in a horse.

—Colonel Grangerford, in *Huckleberry Finn*, 1884, ch. 18

GERMAN

Mark Twain had a terrible time learning how to speak German, and ultimately he decided it was the fault of the German language. His brain rebelled against the unreasonable demands of "the language which enables a man to travel all day in one sentence without changing cars."

"I can *understand* German as well as the maniac that invented it," said Twain, "but I *talk* it best through an interpreter."

One time during a visit to Germany with his friend the Reverend Joe Twichell, Twain was talking about some rather private matters to Twichell within earshot of some Germans, and Twichell became nervous about it.

"Speak in German, Mark," urged Twichell. "Some of these people may understand English."

I was trying to explain to St. Peter, and was doing it in the German tongue, because I didn't want to be too explicit.

—Paine, *Mark Twain's Speeches*, 1923, p. 247

Whenever the literary German dives into a sentence, that is the last you are going to see of him till he emerges on the other side of the Atlantic with his verb in his mouth.

—*A Connecticut Yankee*, 1889, ch. 22

GERMANS

The Germans are exceedingly fond of Rhine wines; they are put up in tall, slender bottles, and are considered a pleasant beverage. One tells them from vinegar by the label.

—*A Tramp Abroad,* 1880, vol. 1, ch. 15

GIFTS

At a Christmas party, a young lady was introduced to Mark Twain and, feeling obligated to discuss literary matters, she asked him if he thought a book was the most useful gift one could give.

His answer was not what she expected. "Yes, but of course it depends on the book. A big leather-bound volume makes an ideal razorstrap. A thin book is useful to stick under a table with a broken caster to steady it. A large, flat atlas can be used to cover a window with a broken pane. And a thick, old-fashioned heavy book with a clasp is the finest thing in the world to throw at a noisy cat."

GIRLS

Philosophers dispute whether it is the promise of what she will be . . . that makes her attractive, the undeveloped maidenhood, or the natural, careless sweetness of childhood.

—*The Gilded Age,* 1873, ch. 6

They say God made man in his effigy. I don't know about that, but I'm quite sure that he put a lot of divinity into the American girl.

—Fisher, *Abroad with Mark Twain,*
1922, p. 212

GOD

In the early 1900s, when the elderly Mark Twain was living in New York City, he received many visitors who came to pay their respects to an American sage. One time, a lady caller asked if she could kiss his hand. Twain's companion, Albert Bigelow Paine, was nonplussed, but the old author graciously accepted the kiss with complete dignity.

"How God must love you!" exclaimed the lady as she was leaving.

"I hope so," replied Twain gently. After she had departed, he turned to Paine and said wistfully, "I guess she hasn't heard of our strained relations."

Mark Twain was not the heretical atheist he was sometimes accused of being. He believed in God, but not the orthodox God of religious tradition. He wrote in his private notebook in 1898, "The Being who to me is the real God is the One who created this majestic universe and rules it. He is the only originator, the only originator of thoughts; thoughts suggested from within, not from without. . . . He is the only creator. He is the perfect artisan, the perfect artist."

Mark Twain believed that to know God was to know Nature. The ways of God are the ways of Nature and can be observed in the natural world. In the introduction to *Letters from the Earth*, he affirmed his doctrine that divine law is natural law:

"Natural Law is the LAW OF GOD—interchangeable names for one and the same thing."

I believe that our Heavenly Father invented Man because he was disappointed in the monkey.

—DeVoto, *Mark Twain in Eruption*,
1940, p. 372

There are many scapegoats for our blunders, but the most popular one is Providence.

—Notebook, 1898

We have infinite trouble in solving man-made mysteries; it is only when we set out to discover the secret of God that our difficulties disappear.

—"As Concerns Interpreting the Deity," essay, 1917

Who gave his angels eternal happiness unearned, yet required his other children to earn it?

—"The Mysterious Stranger," story, 1916, ch. 11

87

The first time the Deity came down to earth, he brought life and death; when he came the second time, he brought hell.

—Satan, in DeVoto, *Letters from the Earth*, 1962, Letter 10

In time, the Deity perceived that death was a mistake—it allowed the dead person to escape from all further persecution in the blessed refuge of the grave. This was not satisfactory. A way must be contrived to pursue the dead beyond the tomb. . . . He invented Hell, and proclaimed it.

—Satan, in DeVoto, *Letters from the Earth*, 1962, Letter 10

Blasphemy? No, it is not blasphemy. If God is as vast as that, he is above blasphemy; if He is as little as that, He is beneath it.

—Paine, *Mark Twain: A Biography*, 1912, vol. 3, p. 1354

Humor must be one of the chief attributes of God. Plants and animals that are distinctly humorous in form and characteristics are God's jokes.

—Paine, *Mark Twain: A Biography*, 1912, vol. 3, p. 1556

Humbly we praise and glorify many of Thy works, and are grateful for their presence in our earth, but not all of them.

—"The Intelligence of God," essay, 1905

God puts *something* good and lovable in every man His hands create.

—"The American Vandal," speech, 1868

No man that ever lived has ever done a thing to please God—primarily. It was done to please himself, *then* God next.

—Paine, *Mark Twain: A Biography*, 1912, vol. 2, p. 1083

GOLF

Golf is a good walk spoiled.

—Attributed

GOOD AND EVIL

Be good and you will be lonesome.

—*Following the Equator,* 1897
(caption for author's photo)

There's a good spot tucked away somewhere in everybody. You'll be a long time finding it, sometimes.

—"Refuge of the Derelicts," story, 1905

Half of the results of a good intention are evil; half the results of an evil intention are good.

—"The Dervish and the Offensive
Stranger," essay, 1923

Such tendency toward doing good as is in men's hearts would not be diminished by the removal of the delusion that good deeds are primarily for the sake of No. 2 instead of for the sake of No. 1.

—"What Is Man?" essay, 1906

To be good is noble; but to show others how to be good is nobler and no trouble.

—*Following the Equator,* 1897, flyleaf

GOSSIP

There is a lot to say in her favor, but the other is more interesting.

—Attributed

GOSSIP COLUMN

Mark Twain is credited with having coined the term "gossip column." The first known use of the term is found in this passage from the story "The Million-Pound Bank Note," published in 1893:

> I had become one of the notorieties of the metropolis of the world. . . . You could not take up a newspaper, English, Scotch, or Irish, without finding in it one or more references to the "vest-pocket million-pounder" and his latest doings and sayings. At first, in these mentions, I was at the bottom of the personal gossip column; next, I was listed above the knights, next above the barons, and so on.

GOVERNMENT

Mark Twain was sometimes cynical about public officials, as when he offered this definition: "Public servants: Persons chosen by the people to distribute the graft."

But beneath his gruff disenchantment with the politicians of his time lay a deep love of democracy and a profound desire to preserve American liberty against all encroachments. He preferred the vices of democracy to the crimes of monarchy and despotism. "There never was a throne which did not represent a crime," he wrote. "Despotism is not merely a bad form of government, it is the worst form that is possible."

Although it was Mark Twain who invented the term "New Deal," which is associated with an expanded role of government, he nevertheless warned against the unchecked growth of Big Government: "The mania for giving the Government power to meddle with the private affairs of cities or citizens is likely to cause endless trouble."

He urged Americans to exercise their power to vote and "make unhampered choice and bless Heaven that they live in a free land where no form of despotism can ever intrude."

Mark Twain was proud to be an American and contended that the American government, with all its flaws and follies, was the best and fairest ever devised. "I think I can say, and say with pride," he declared in a Fourth of July speech in 1873, "that we have some legislatures that bring higher prices than any in the world."

In statesmanship get the formalities right, never mind about the moralities.

—*Following the Equator,* 1897, vol. 2, ch. 29

That's the difference between governments and individuals. Governments don't care, individuals do.

—*A Tramp Abroad,* 1880, vol. 2, ch. 10

"Our Country, right or wrong . . ." Have you not perceived that that phrase is an insult to the nation? . . . Only when a republic's life is in danger should a man uphold his government when it is in the wrong. There is no other time. This republic's life is not in peril.

—"Glances at History," in DeVoto,
Letters from the Earth, 1962

No country can be well governed unless its citizens as a body keep religiously before their minds that they are the guardians of the law, and that the law officers are only the machinery for its execution, nothing more.

—*The Gilded Age,* 1873, ch. 39

GRANT, ULYSSES S.

In 1880, Ulysses S. Grant came to Hartford to speak, and Mark Twain was delegated to make an introductory speech of welcome to the former President. "Your country stands ready from this day forth to testify her measureless love and pride and gratitude toward you," Twain pledged from the podium, "in every conceivable *inexpensive* way."

Grant was a grim-faced man who did not laugh often or easily, but on hearing the word "inexpensive," he broke up completely, and laughed until his eyes filled with tears.

GREATNESS

Greatness may be classed as the ability to win recognition.

—Read, *Mark Twain and I,* 1940, p. 11

GRIEF

It is one of the mysteries of our nature that a man, all unprepared, can receive a thunder-stroke like that and live. There is but one reasonable explanation of it. The intellect is stunned by the shock and but gropingly gathers the meaning of the words. The power to realize their full import is mercifully wanting.

—On receiving a telegram of his
daughter Susy's death, August 1896

Nothing that grieves us can be called little: by the eternal laws of proportion a child's loss of a doll and a king's loss of a crown are events of the same size.

—"Which Was the Dream?" story,
1897

GROWTH

What is the most rigorous law of our being? Growth. No smallest atom of our moral, mental, or physical structure can stand still a year. It grows—it must grow; nothing can prevent it.

—"Consistency," speech, 1887

GRUESOME

An elderly woman approached Mark Twain after a lecture and said, "I'm just reading *Life on the Mississippi*. Some of the episodes are so gruesome!"

"Incidents that horrify some may provide relief to others," replied Twain. "It reminds me of Ed Johnson, a sheriff down in Arkansas. During logging season sometimes a body would come floating down the river. One day the deputies brought ashore a particularly well-dressed corpse. Sheriff Johnson searched one of the victim's pockets and found a $20 bill. In another pocket he found a pistol. 'That's too bad,' he said, shaking his head. 'I'm going to have to fine this man $20 for carrying this pistol.' "

GUEST

Mark Twain was a difficult guest to have around the house. "It is irksome to me to behave myself," he explained. "I had rather call on people who know me and will kindly leave me entirely unrestrained, and simply employ themselves in looking out for the spoons."

Few hosts met Mark Twain's strict standards, and so he preferred to be a guest in a hotel rather than a private house. "When I am ill-natured, I so enjoy the freedom of a hotel—where I can ring up a domestic and give him a quarter and then break furniture over him—then I go to bed calmed and sleep as peacefully as a child."

GUNS

In Mark Twain's time, newspapers frequently ran stories about fatal mishaps with guns, and young people customarily received many stern warnings about the hazards of playing with firearms. Mimicking these admonitions in his 1882 address "Advice to Youth," Twain cautioned young people to beware that unloaded weapons were harmless *except* in the vicinity of relatives: "A youth who can't hit a cathedral at thirty yards with a Gatling gun in three-quarters of an hour, can take up an empty old musket and bag his grandmother every time."

It appeared to me to be a dangerous weapon. It had only one fault—you could not hit anything with it. One of our "conductors" practiced awhile on a cow with it, and as long as she stood still and behaved herself she was safe; but as soon as she went to moving about, and he got to shooting at other things, she came to grief.

—*Roughing It,* 1872, ch. 1

And the next instant he was one of the deadest men that ever lived.

—*Roughing It,* 1872, ch. 10
(of a victim of the notorious
gunfighter Slade)

HABITS

Nothing so needs reforming as other people's habits.

—Pudd'nhead Wilson, 1894, ch. 15

Habit is habit, and not to be flung out of the window by any man, but coaxed downstairs a step at a time.

—Pudd'nhead Wilson, 1894, ch. 6

The widder eats by a bell; she goes to bed by a bell; she gits up by a bell—everything's so awful reg'lar a body can't stand it.

—Tom Sawyer, 1876, ch. 35
(Huck referring to the Widow
Douglas's civilized habits)

A man may have no bad habits and have worse.

—Following the Equator, 1897, vol. 1, ch. 1

HAIR

When red headed people are above a certain social grade their hair is auburn.

—*A Connecticut Yankee*, 1889, ch. 18

HALLEY'S COMET

"I came in with Halley's Comet in 1835," Mark Twain told his biographer Albert Bigelow Paine in 1909. "It is coming again next year, and I expect to go out with it. It will be the greatest disappointment of my life if I don't go out with Halley's Comet. The Almighty has said, no doubt: 'Now here are these two unaccountable freaks; they came in together, they must go out together.' Oh! I am looking forward to that."

As fate would have it, it happened just that way, just as Mark Twain wanted it. He was born on November 30, 1835, only two weeks after the perihelion of Halley's Comet on its only visit of the nineteenth century. He died on April 21, 1910, the day after the perihelion of Halley's Comet on its first visit of the twentieth century.

HANDSOME

Twenty-four years ago I was strangely handsome; in San Francisco in the rainy season I was often mistaken for fair weather.

—Attributed

HAPPINESS

Happiness ain't a *thing in itself*—it's only a *contrast* with something that ain't pleasant.

—"Captain Stormfield's Visit to Heaven," story, 1907

As soon as the novelty is over and the force of contrast dulled, it ain't happiness any longer, and you have to get something fresh.

—"Captain Stormfield's Visit to Heaven," story, 1907

Are you so unobservant as not to have found out that sanity and happiness are an impossible combination?

> —Satan, in "The Mysterious
> Stranger," story, 1916, ch. 10

To be *busy* is man's only happiness.

> —Letter to his brother, Orion
> Clemens, February 21, 1868

Happiness is a Swedish sunset—it is there for all, but most of us look the other way and lose it.

> —Notebook, 1899

HAT

It is hazardous to wear another person's hat. In a Fourth of July speech in London in 1899, Mark Twain described how he had mistakenly picked up the hat of an Anglican churchman, Canon Wilberforce.

Recalling the incident with a mixture of awe and wonder, Twain confessed, "I was for five hours under so strong a clerical influence that I could not tell a lie."

HAWAII

It is paradise for an indolent man.

> —"The Sandwich Islands," speech, 1866

At noon I observed a bevy of nude native young ladies bathing in the sea, and went and sat down on their clothes to keep them from being stolen.

> —*Roughing It*, 1872, ch. 72

How sad it is to think of the multitudes who have gone to their graves in this beautiful island and never knew there was a hell!

> —*Roughing It*, 1872, ch. 67
> (of the natives of pre-Christian
> Hawaii)

HEADACHES

Do not undervalue the headache. While it is at its sharpest it seems a bad investment; but when relief begins, the unexpired remainder is worth four dollars a minute.

—*Following the Equator*, 1897, vol. 2, ch. 18

HEALTH

"Be careful about reading health books," warned Mark Twain. "You may die of a misprint."

Mark Twain's health regimen was a simple one. Whenever he fell ill he would give up his vices, such as smoking and drinking, until his health returned. Then he took up his vices again. He found that this system of health maintenance worked well for him but would not work for everybody. He once recommended it to an ailing old lady, but she had insufficient vices.

"She said she could not stop swearing and smoking and drinking, because she had never done these things. So there it was. She had neglected her habits, and hadn't any. Now that they would have come good, there were none in stock. She had nothing to fall back on. She was a sinking vessel, with no freight in her to throw overboard. . . . Why, even one or two little bad habits could have saved her, but she was just a moral pauper."

There are people who strictly deprive themselves of each and every eatable, drinkable and smokable which has in any way acquired a shady reputation. They pay this price for health. And health is all they get for it. How strange it is. It is like paying out your whole fortune for a cow that has gone dry.

—Neider, *Autobiography*, 1959, ch. 2

The only way to keep your health is to eat what you don't want, drink what you don't like, and do what you'd druther not.

—*Following the Equator*, 1897, vol. 2, ch. 13

Under our free institutions anybody can poison himself that wants to and will pay the price.

—Neider, *Autobiography*, 1959, ch. 51

HEALTH SPA

Mark Twain once spent a dreary week at a German health spa, where the principal topic of conversation was not life but the liver.

"Wherever you see two or a dozen people of ordinary bulk talking together, you know they are talking about their livers. When you first arrive here your new acquaintances seem sad and hard to talk to, but pretty soon you get the lay of the land and the hand of things, and after that you haven't any more trouble. You look into the dreary dull eye and softly say:

" 'Well, how's your liver?'

"You will see that dim eye flash up with a grateful flame, and you will see that jaw begin to work, and you will recognize that nothing is required of you from this out but to listen as long as you remain conscious."

HEART

It is in the heart that the values lie. I wish I could make him understand that a loving heart is riches, and riches enough, and that without it intellect is poverty.

—Eve, in "Eve's Diary," story, 1905

Civilizations proceed from the heart rather than from the head.

—Letter to Alvert Sonnichsen, 1901

You can't reason with your heart; it has its own laws, and thumps about things which the intellect scorns.

—*A Connecticut Yankee,* 1889, ch. 20

The heart is the real Fountain of Youth.

—Notebook, 1898

HEAVEN

One of the last things Mark Twain wrote, only a few days before his death, was a squib of humorous "Advice" on how to behave properly upon arrival at the Pearly Gates of Heaven. Among his pointers for pilgrims:

> Upon arrival do not speak to St. Peter until spoken to.
> Do not begin any remark with, "Say."
> Leave your dog outside. Heaven goes by favor. If it went by
> merit you would stay out and the dog would go in.

Mark Twain did not believe in the conventional Christian heaven, the last resort of the good. When he heard preachers talk about it, he felt like Huckleberry Finn listening to Miss Watson: "She went on and told me all about the good place. She said all a body would have to do there was to go around all day long with a harp and sing, forever and ever. So I didn't think much of it."

As the practical Captain Stormfield discovers in his visit to heaven, "Singing hymns and waving palm branches through all eternity is pretty when you hear about it in the pulpit, but it's as poor a way to put in valuable time as a body could contrive."

Twain asserted that whether a man went to heaven or hell, it would seem like hell. "He will think he is in hell anyhow, no matter which place he goes to; because in the good place you pro-gress, pro-gress, pro-gress—study, study, study, all the time—and if this isn't hell I don't know what is."

We may not doubt that society in heaven consists mainly of undesirable persons.

—Notebook, 1902

There is no humor in heaven.

—"Captain Stormfield's Visit to
Heaven," story, 1907

Let us swear while we may, for in heaven it will not be allowed.

—Notebook, 1898

HELL

Heaven for climate, hell for society.

—"Tammany and Croker," speech,
1901

When I reflect upon the number of disagreeable people who I know have gone to a better world, I am moved to lead a different life.

—*Pudd'nhead Wilson*, 1894, ch. 13

Oh, I know how you feel! I've been in hell myself.

—Letter to William Dean Howells,
October 19, 1899

HERESY

One of Mark Twain's quips that earned him a reputation for heresy was his remark on the impossibility of a Second Advent in Palestine. Twain argued that the Savior, having been there once, would surely never return to so dismal a country. When word of this blasphemy was heard in San Francisco, a local clergyman delivered a homily against "this son of the devil, Mark Twain."

Sometimes I feel like the sane person in a community of the mad; sometimes I feel like the one blind man where all others see; the one groping savage in the college of the learned, and always, during service, I feel like a heretic in heaven.

—"At the Shrine of St. Wagner,"
essay, 1891

HEROES

We find not much in ourselves to admire, we are always privately wanting to be like somebody else. If everybody was satisfied with himself there would be no heroes.

—Neider, *Autobiography*, 1959, ch. 52

We admire them, we envy them, for great qualities which we ourselves lack. Hero worship consists in just that.

—Neider, *Autobiography*, 1959, ch. 52

That a person can really be a hero to a near and familiar friend is a thing which no hero has ever yet been able to realize.

—Neider, *Autobiography*, 1959, ch. 16

HEROINE

Heroine: girl who is perfectly charming to live with, in a book.

—Johnson, *More Maxims of Mark*, 1927,
p. 8

HEROISM

Heroism tends to increase with the telling. In his steamboat days, Mark Twain often found himself in the company of tall-talking men who never tired of telling tales of their own heroic exploits. When it came his turn, Twain once offered this contribution:

"There was a fire in Hannibal one night, and old man Hankinson got caught in the fourth story of the burning house. It looked as if the old man was a goner. None of the ladders were long enough to reach him. Nobody knew what to do. Nobody could think of anything. Nobody had any presence of mind—nobody but me.

"I was forced to take action myself. 'Fetch a rope,' I yelled, 'somebody fetch a rope.' When the rope came, I threw the old man the end of it. He caught it. 'Tie it around your waist!' I instructed him. He did so, and I pulled him down."

HINDUISM

It is a good and gentle religion, but inconvenient.

—*Following the Equator*, 1897, vol. 2, ch. 13

HISTORY

The very ink with which all history is written is merely fluid prejudice.

—*Following the Equator*, 1897, vol. 2, ch. 33

By the Law of Periodical Repetition, everything which has happened once must happen again.

> —"Papers of the Adam Family," in
> DeVoto, *Letters from the Earth*, 1962

A historian who would convey the truth has got to lie. Often he must enlarge the truth by diameters, otherwise his reader would not be able to see it.

> —Paine, *Mark Twain: A Biography*,
> 1912, vol. 3, p. 1514

HOLY GRAIL

Every year expeditions went out holy grailing, and next year relief expeditions went out to hunt for *them*. There was worlds of reputation in it, but no money.

> —*A Connecticut Yankee*, 1889, ch. 9

HONESTY

"Did you ever try to make yourself believe a lie, Mark?" an old friend named Ellis Grimp asked him.

"Yes," answered Mark Twain. "When I sought to convince myself that certain politicians were honest."

"Did you ever meet a man that was absolutely honest?"

"Yes, I think so."

"And did you talk with him?"

"Well, hardly. He hadn't been honest but a short time," said Mark Twain. "I was attending his funeral."

There are people who think that honesty is always the best policy. This is a superstition: there are times when the appearance of it is worth six of it.

> —Attributed

Barring that natural expression of villainy which we all have, the man looked honest enough.

> —"A Mysterious Visit," sketch, 1875

It is my belief that there isn't a single male human being in America who is honest.

—Neider, *Autobiography*, 1959, ch. 24

Honesty: the best of all the lost arts.

—Notebook, 1902

When a merely honest man appears he is a comet—his fame is eternal—needs no genius, no talent—mere honesty—Luther, Christ, etc.

—Notebook, 1885

Yes, even I am dishonest. Not in many ways, but in some. Forty-one, I think it is.

—Letter to Joe Twichell, March 14,
1905

HONORS

It is better to deserve honors and not have them than to have them and not deserve them.

—Notebook, 1902

The cross of the Legion of Honor has been conferred upon me. However, few escape that distinction.

—*A Tramp Abroad*, 1880, vol. 1, ch. 8

It pleased me beyond measure when Yale made me a Master of Arts, because I didn't know anything about art. . . . I rejoiced again when Missouri University made me a Doctor of Laws, because it was all clear profit, I not knowing anything about laws except how to evade them. . . . And now at Oxford I am to be made a Doctor of Letters—all clear profit, because what I don't know about letters would make me a multi-millionaire if I could turn it into cash.

—Neider, *Autobiography*, 1959, ch. 73

HORSES

In *Roughing It,* Mark Twain tells how he bought his first horse. It was at an auction in Carson City, Nevada. When a particularly uncomely creature was offered for sale, a man standing nearby said to Twain, "He is, without the shadow of a doubt, a Genuine Mexican Plug!"

Mark Twain did not know what a Genuine Mexican Plug was, "but there was something about this man's way of saying it that made me swear inwardly that I would own a Genuine Mexican Plug, or die."

Twain bought the horse, and did not find out till later that the man who had spoken was the auctioneer's brother. The horse bucked wildly, discarded its rider, then "darted away like a telegram. He soared over three fences like a bird and disappeared down the road."

Twain was hurt by this experience, in more ways than one. "I made up my mind that if the auctioneer's brother's funeral took place while I was in the Territory I would postpone all other recreations and attend it."

The minute I was in the saddle I was up in the air, and up and up. . . . When I came down he was gone. I have not practiced any horsemanship since. It was a valuable lesson I learned. I have been able to avoid horsemanship ever since, and it has probably saved my life.

—"Caprices of Memory," speech,
1908

HOTELS

Mark Twain once considered opening a hotel of his own, so that he might receive dollars in exchange for offering quarters. He even prepared a set of rules and regulations for "Mark Twain's Hotel," which were published in a Downieville, California, newspaper in 1877. Some of the rules are appended here:

This house will be considered strictly intemperate.
None but the brave deserve the fare.
Boarders who do not wish to pay in advance are requested
to advance and pay.

Persons owing bills for board will be bored for bills.

Double boarders can have two beds with a room in it, or two rooms with a bed in it, as they choose.

Single men and their families will not be boarded.

Dreams will be charged for by the dozen.

Stone vaults will be hired to snoring boarders, and the proprieter will in no wise be responsible for the broken tympanums of others.

It is an art apart. Saint Francis of Assisi said, "All saints can do miracles, but few of them can keep hotel."

—Notebook, 1898

It used to be a good hotel, but that proves nothing—I used to be a good boy.

—*Innocents Abroad,* 1869, vol. 2, ch. 57

We tarried overnight at . . . The Grand Hotel. . . . There was nothing grand about it but the bill.

—"Letters to Satan," *Europe and Elsewhere,* 1923

HOUSE

The house is full of carpenters and decorators whereas, what we really need here, is an incendiary.

—Letter to Charles Stoddard, October 26, 1881

The house was as empty as a beer closet in premises where painters have been at work.

—"McWilliamses and the Burglar Alarm," story, 1882

The partitions of the houses were so thin we could hear the women occupants of adjoining rooms changing their minds.

—Johnson, *Remembered Yesterdays,* 1923, p. 324

There ought to be a room in this house to swear in. It's dangerous to have to repress an emotion like that.

—Paine, *Mark Twain: A Biography,*
1912, vol. 3, p. 1301

HOUSEKEEPING

That kind of so-called housekeeping where they have six bottles and no corkscrew.

—Notebook, 1890

HUCKLEBERRY FINN

He was the only really independent person—boy or man—in the community, and by consequence he was tranquilly and continuously happy and was envied by all the rest of us.

—Neider, *Autobiography,* 1959, ch. 14
(of Tom Blankenship, real-life model
for Huckleberry Finn)

HUMAN BEING

Human beings seem to be a poor invention. If they are the noblest works of God where is the ignoblest?

—Notebook, 1896

HUMAN NATURE

We are all alike—on the inside.

—"Andrew Carnegie," in DeVoto,
Mark Twain in Eruption, 1940

From his cradle to his grave a man never does a single thing which has any first and foremost object but one—to secure peace of mind, spiritual comfort, for himself.

—"What Is Man?" essay, 1906

I have no race prejudices, and I think I have no color prejudices or caste prejudices nor creed prejudices. Indeed I know it. I can stand any society. All that I care to know is that a man is a human being—that is enough for me; he can't be any worse.

—"Concerning the Jews," essay, 1899

Such is the human race. Often it does seem such a pity that Noah didn't miss the boat.

—*Christian Science*, 1907, bk. 2, ch. 7

The last quarter of a century of my life has been pretty constantly and faithfully devoted to the study of the human race—that is to say, the study of myself, for in my individual person I am the entire human race compacted together. I have found that there is no ingredient of the race which I do not possess in either a small way or a large way.

—Neider, *Autobiography*, 1959, ch. 26

It is governed by minorities, seldom or never by majorities. It suppresses its feelings and its beliefs and follows the handful that makes the most noise. Sometimes the noisy handful is right, sometimes wrong; but no matter, the crowd follows it.

—"The Mysterious Stranger," story, 1916, ch. 9

Monarchies, aristocracies, and religions are all based upon that large defect in your race—the individual's distrust of his neighbor, and his desire, for safety's or comfort's sake, to stand well in his neighbor's eye.

—"The Mysterious Stranger," story, 1916, ch. 9

There it is: it doesn't make any difference who we are or what we are, there's always *somebody* to look down on.

—"3,000 Years Among the Microbes," story, 1905

HUMILITY

There's a breed of humility which is *itself* a species of showing off.

—"The Esquimau Maiden's
Romance," story, 1893

HUMOR

Against the assault of laughter nothing can stand.

—"The Mysterious Stranger," story,
1916, ch. 10

Everything human is pathetic. The secret source of Humor itself is not joy but sorrow. There is no humor in heaven.

—*Following the Equator,* 1897, vol. 1, ch. 10

Humor must not professedly teach and it must not professedly preach, but it must do both if it would live forever.

—Neider, *Autobiography,* 1959, ch. 55

Laughter without a tinge of philosophy is but a sneeze of humor. Genuine humor is replete with wisdom.

Read, *Mark Twain and I,* 1940, p. 17

The humorous story is told gravely; the teller does his best to conceal the fact that he even dimly suspects that there is anything funny about it.

—"How to Tell a Story," essay, 1895

The humorous story is American, the comic story is English, the witty story is French. The humorous story depends for its effect upon the *manner* of the telling; the comic story and the witty story upon the *matter.*

—"How to Tell a Story," essay, 1895

To string incongruities and absurdities together in a wandering and sometimes purposeless way, and seem innocently unaware

that they are absurdities, is the basis of the American art, if my
position is correct. Another feature is the slurring of the point. A
third is the dropping of a studied remark apparently without
knowing it, as if one were thinking aloud. The fourth and the last
is the pause.

—"How to Tell a Story," essay, 1895

Repetition is a mighty power in the domain of humor. If frequently used, nearly any precisely worded and unchanging for-
mula will eventually compel laughter if it be gravely and earnestly
repeated, at intervals, five or six times.

—Neider, *Autobiography*, 1959, ch. 28

Humor is the great thing, the saving thing, after all. The minute
it crops up, all our hardnesses yield, all our irritations and resent-
ments flit away, and a sunny spirit takes their place.

—"What Paul Bourget Thinks of Us,"
essay, 1895

The funniest things are the forbidden.

—Notebook, 1879

Humor is mankind's greatest blessing.

—Paine, *Mark Twain: A Biography*,
1912, vol. 3, p. 1556

HUMORISTS

The greatest American humorist before Mark Twain's advent was
Artemus Ward. Though the two men belonged to different generations, they became good friends nevertheless.

Mark Twain recalled how Artemus Ward once said to him
seriously, "Clemens, I have done too much fooling, too much
trifling; I am going to write something that will live."

"Well, what, for instance?" Twain asked.

Ward looked at him solemnly and replied, "A lie."

Humorists of the "mere" sort cannot survive.

—Neider, *Autobiography*, 1959, ch. 55

To simply amuse them would have satisfied my dearest ambition at any time; for they could get instruction elsewhere and I had two chances to help to the teacher's one: for amusement is a good preparation for study and a good healer of fatigue after it.

—Letter to Andrew Lang, 1890

The humorous writer professes to awaken and direct your love, your pity, your kindness—your scorn for untruth, pretension, imposture. . . . He takes upon himself to be the week-day preacher.

—"Notes on Thackeray's Essay on Swift," undated

HUNTING

During the administration of Theodore Roosevelt, the President made headlines with his weekend hunting prowess. One time, the Great Hunter was reported to have bagged a bear, but Mark Twain was profoundly skeptical. He believed the President had bagged a cow.

"I am sure he honestly thinks it was a bear," wrote Twain, "but the circumstantial evidence that it was a cow is overwhelming. It acted just as a cow would act—it even left a cow track behind, which is what a cow would do."

Twain believed Roosevelt's ostentatious hunting behavior was symptomatic of an immature mind. He called Teddy Roosevelt "a great big boy," and added, "A grown person would have milked the cow and let her go."

HYPOCRISY

A hypocritical businessman, whose fortune had been the misfortune of many others, told Mark Twain piously, "Before I die I intend to make a pilgrimage to the Holy Land. I want to climb to the top of Mount Sinai and read the Ten Commandments aloud."

"I have a better idea," suggested Twain. "Why don't you stay right at home in Boston and keep them?"

What a hell of a heaven it will be when they get all these hypocrites assembled there!

—Letter to Joe Twichell, January 29, 1901

IDEAS

The man with a new idea is a Crank until the idea succeeds.

—Following the Equator, 1897, vol. 1, ch. 32

The fact is the human race is not only slow about borrowing valuable ideas—it sometimes persists in not borrowing them at all.

—"Some National Stupidities," essay, 1923

I think that as a rule we develop a borrowed European idea forward and that Europe develops a borrowed American idea backwards.

—"Some National Stupidities," essay, 1923

It always happens that when a man seizes upon a neglected and important idea, people inflamed with the same notion crop up all around.

—*Life on the Mississippi*, 1883, ch. 1

You've got to admire men that deal in ideas of that size and can tote them around without crutches.

—*Life on the Mississippi*, 1883, ch. 28

IDEALS

It is at our mother's knee that we acquire our noblest and truest and highest ideals, but there is seldom any money in them.

—Paine, *Mark Twain: A Biography*, 1912, vol. 3, p. 1513

IGNORANCE

I would rather have my ignorance than another man's knowledge, because I have got so much more *of* it.

—Letter to William Dean Howells, February 10, 1875

His ignorance covered the whole earth like a blanket, and there was hardly a hole in it anywhere.

—DeVoto, *Mark Twain in Eruption*, 1940, p. 180

The ignorant are afraid to betray surprise or admiration . . . they think it ill manners.

—*Notebook*, 1883

We never knew an ignorant person yet but was prejudiced.

—*Innocents Abroad*, 1869, ch. 10

That is just the way with some people. They get down on a thing when they don't know nothing about it.

—*Huckleberry Finn*, 1884, ch. 1

ILLUSIONS

Don't part with your illusions. When they are gone you may still exist, but you have ceased to live.

—*Following the Equator,* 1897, vol. 2, ch. 23

IMAGINATION

Against a diseased imagination, demonstration goes for nothing.

—"A Campaign That Failed," story, 1885

You can't depend on your eyes when your imagination is out of focus.

—Notebook, 1898

When a man goes back to look at the house of his childhood, it has always *shrunk:* there is no instance of such a house being as big as the picture in memory and imagination calls for.

—Letter to William Dean Howells, 1887

It's a blessed thing to have an imagination that can always make you satisfied, no matter how you are fixed.

—*The American Claimant,* 1892, ch. 4

IMMORALITY

There is a Moral Sense, and there is an Immoral Sense. History shows us that the Moral Sense enables us to perceive morality and how to avoid it, and that the Immoral Sense enables us to perceive immorality and how to enjoy it.

—*Following the Equator,* 1897, vol. 1, ch. 16

IMMORTALITY

Mark Twain and Samuel Clemens were divided on the question of immortality. The author's dual personality encompassed both the skeptic and the believer, with the result that he made contradictory statements on the subject.

When he discussed immortality with Christians, he usually took the skeptic's point of view, for he relished the role of devil's advocate. He often argued the issue with the preacher Henry Ward Beecher and Mrs. Beecher. One day, Mrs. Beecher found some thin-layered leaves of stone in her garden, and knowing Mark Twain's interest in geology, she showed them to him. He resolved to write an agreement with her on those timeless leaves, to be set aside until the ages should settle the question of immortality. He wrote:

> If you prove right and I prove wrong,
>   A million years from now,
> In language plain and frank and strong,
>   My error I'll avow
> To your dear waking face.
>
> If I prove right, by God His grace,
>   Full sorry I shall be,
> For in that solitude no trace
>   There'll be of you and me.
>
> A million years, O patient stone,
>   You've waited for this message.
> Deliver it a million hence;
>   (Survivor pays expressage.)
>   *Mark Twain*

—Contract with Mrs. T. K. Beecher,
July 2, 1895

One of the proofs of the immortality of the soul is that myriads have believed in it. They have also believed the world was flat.

—Notebook, 1900

I have never seen what to me seemed an atom of proof that there is a future life. And yet—I am strongly inclined to expect one.

—Paine, *Mark Twain: A Biography*,
1912, vol. 3, p. 1431

IMPERIALISM

All the territorial possessions of all the political establishments in the earth—including America, of course—consist of pilferings from other people's wash.

—*Following the Equator,* 1897, vol. 2, ch. 27

By help of these suggested amendments, Progress and Civilization in that country can have a boom, and it will take in the Persons who are Sitting in Darkness, and we can resume Business at the old stand.

—"To the Person Sitting in Darkness," essay, 1901

IMPERSONATORS

There are a number of professional Mark Twain impersonators today, but back in the nineteenth century there was apparently at least one such impersonator who was a con man. Twain referred to him as "The Double." The Double, according to the author, had lectured in various small towns under the name of Mark Twain, collected the fees, and then skipped out on the hotel bills, which were promptly forwarded to the real Mark Twain (Samuel Clemens).

Twain claimed to be painfully embarrassed by the behavior of his double:

"It delivered a lecture in Satan's Delight, Idaho, on 'The Moral Impossibility of Doughnuts,' a subject in which I *never* took the slightest interest in my life." In Wisconsin: "It advertised itself to lecture and didn't; It got supernaturally drunk at other people's expense." Across the Midwest: "It continued Its relentless war upon helpless and unoffending boarding-houses."

While Mark Twain certainly may have embellished the story of his double, historical records suggest that he was plagued by impostors, both in America and abroad.

IMPURITY

To the pure all things are impure.

—Notebook, 1899

INDECENCY

The first thing a missionary teaches a savage is indecency.

—Notebook, 1897

Each race determines for itself what indecencies are. Nature knows no indecencies; man invents them.

—Notebook, 1896

INDECISION

I must have a prodigious quantity of mind; it takes me as much as a week sometimes to make it up.

—*Innocents Abroad,* 1869, ch. 7

INDEPENDENCE

Independence . . . is loyalty to one's best self and principles, and this is often disloyalty to the general idols and fetishes.

—Notebook, 1888

The quality of independence was almost wholly left out of the human race. The scattering exceptions to the rule only emphasize it, light it up, make it glare.

—Paine, *Autobiography,* 1924, vol. 2, p. 9

INDIA

Mark Twain's visit to India, as described in *Following the Equator* (1897), was marred by an unpleasant incident which occurred in Delhi. Wild monkeys invaded the bedroom where he was staying, coming in through the window in the night.

"When I awoke one of them was before the glass brushing his hair and the other one had my note-book, and was reading a page of humorous notes and crying."

Mark Twain was upset by this experience. "I did not mind the one with the hairbrush but the conduct of the other one hurt me."

But an even more harrowing episode occurred in the jungle,

where Mark Twain had a potentially fatal encounter with a cobra. "A cobra bit me," recalled the intrepid author, "but it got well; everyone was surprised. This could not happen twice in ten years, perhaps. Usually death would result in fifteen minutes."

India has two million gods, and worships them all. In religion other countries are paupers; India is the only millionaire.

—*Following the Equator*, 1897, vol. 2, ch. 7

I believe that in India "cold weather" is merely a conventional phrase and has come into use through the necessity of having some way to distinguish between weather which will melt a brass door-knob and weather which will only make it mushy.

—*Following the Equator*, 1897, vol. 2, ch. 18

With her [India] everything is on a giant scale—even her poverty; no other country can show anything to compare with it.

—*Following the Equator*, 1897, vol. 2, ch. 7

INDUSTRY

When Samuel Clemens was an ambitious young lad, he was deeply impressed by the story of an industrious boy who became a millionaire. What stuck in Clemens's memory was that the boy's big break came when the lad was noticed by a wealthy business-man in the act of picking up a pin from the sidewalk.

At the age of eighteen, Samuel Clemens left Hannibal and went to New York to seek his fortune, or at least employment of some kind. Remembering the story of the industrious boy, he chose a good location in front of an office window and began picking up pins which he had surreptitiously strewn about on the sidewalk. After half an hour of this, one of the men in the office came out to speak with him. But instead of offering him either praise or employment, the man said, "You! Haven't you anything better to do than pick up pins off the street? You must be an utterly worthless fool!"

From the beginning of my sojourn in this world there was a persistent vacancy in me where the industry ought to be.

—Neider, *Autobiography*, 1959, ch. 30

INSANITY

Really, what we want now, is not laws against crime, but a law against *insanity*. That is where the true evil lies.

—"A New Crime," essay, 1875

Another thing which we often forget—or try to: that no man has a wholly undiseased mind; that in one way or another all men are mad.

—"The Memorable Assassination,"
essay, 1917

The way it is now, the asylums can hold the sane people, but if we tried to shut up the insane we should run out of building materials.

—*Following the Equator*, 1897, vol. 2, ch. 14

The human race consists of the dangerously insane and such as are not.

—Notebook, 1902

INSULTS

When Mark Twain disapproved of someone, he was not likely to keep it a secret. A remark he made on hearing of the death of an annoying person is typical:

"He has done a thing for me which I wouldn't even have done for myself. If he will only stay dead now I will call the account square and drop the grudge I bear him."

The dead are accustomed to flattering eulogies, but not from Mark Twain. "He is dead and buried now, though; let him rest, let him rot," he wrote of one particular corpse. "Let his vices be forgotten, but his virtues be remembered; it will not infringe much upon any man's time."

Some of Mark Twain's insults have become classics. One of

his comments about a California leader of the 1860s—"a solemn, unsmiling, sanctimonious old iceberg that looked like he was waiting for a vacancy on the Trinity"—was later taken up by H. L. Mencken and applied to Woodrow Wilson with devastating effect.

Twain was unforgiving of fools, describing one in particular as being "endowed with a stupidity which by the least little stretch would go around the globe four times and tie."

The fair sex was not indemnified against Mark Twain. Of a stout lady in society, he wrote: "She appeared as if she had been through one famine and got about two-thirds through another." Of a lady who would not admit her age, he observed: "She was old enough to be a great-grandmother to Mary that had the little lamb." Of a prominent termagant, he said: "I do not believe I could ever learn to like her except on a raft at sea with no other provisions in sight."

Mark Twain did not spare the rich and powerful. Of Cecil Rhodes, he took note: "I admire him. I frankly confess it; and when his time comes I shall buy a piece of the rope for a keepsake."

The great masters of art were not insured against Mark Twain: "I never felt so fervently thankful, so soothed, so tranquil," he wrote in *Innocents Abroad,* "so filled with a blessed peace as I did yesterday when I learned that Michelangelo was dead."

Nor did he spare the sacred and the holy. "Of all the lands there are for dismal scenery, I think Palestine must be the prince," he declared in that notorious travel book. "It is a hopeless, dreary, heart-broken land." Then he made his infamous quip that the Second Coming would not occur there because Christ, having been once, would never come back.

Neither was native American religion exempt from the wrath of Twain. He described the Mormon Bible as "chloroform in print. If Joseph Smith composed this book, the act was a miracle—keeping awake while he did it was, at any rate."

American government received its fair share of abuse: "Suppose you were an idiot. And suppose you were a member of Congress. But I repeat myself."

The American educational system also received its due: "In the first place God made idiots. This was for practice. Then He made School Boards."

But what the democratic Mark Twain despised more than anything else, probably, was monarchy and royalty. When the shah of Persia came to visit America in 1873, Twain reported it for the *New York Herald*. While others gave the shah the royal treatment, Twain described him as "a man who has never done anything to win our gratitude or excite our admiration except that he managed to starve a million of his subjects to death in twelve months. If he had starved the rest I suppose we would set up a monument to him now."

Mark Twain reserved some of his most scathing remarks for other writers whom he believed to be overrated, such as James Fenimore Cooper, Henry James, George Eliot, and Jane Austen. Once, when he noticed the absence of Austen's books from a ship's library, he commented: "Just that one omission alone would make a fairly good library out of a library that hadn't a book in it." On another occasion, he said of Jane: "It seems a great pity that they allowed her to die a natural death."

In response to a statement that the writer Walter Scott would outlive all his critics, Mark Twain conceded the point. "The fact of the business is, you've got to be one of two ages to appreciate Scott. When you're eighteen you can read *Ivanhoe*, and you want to wait until you are ninety to read some of the rest. It takes a pretty well-regulated abstemious critic to live 90 years."

Of a much-praised book by Henry James, he observed: "Once you put it down, you simply can't pick it up."

But it was Fenimore Cooper who took Twain's toughest punches in the literary arena. The essay "Fenimore Cooper's Literary Offenses" may be the most devastating piece of literary criticism ever written, and is certainly the funniest. "Cooper has scored 114 offenses against literary art out of a possible 115. It breaks the record."

Mark Twain was not a man to hold a grudge, however, at least not for more than a quarter of a century. In his heart he was always able to find forgiveness, even for his first publisher, Elisha Bliss, who had swindled him. "He has been dead a quarter of a century now. My bitterness against him has faded away and disappeared. I feel only compassion for him and if I could send him a fan I would."

He is useless on top of the ground; he ought to be under it, inspiring the cabbages.

—*Pudd'nhead Wilson,* 1894, ch. 21

You take the lies out of him, and he'll shrink to the size of your hat; you take the malice out of him, and he'll disappear.

—*Life on the Mississippi,* 1883, ch. 24

It was not lively enough for a pleasure trip; but if we had only had a corpse it would have made a noble funeral excursion.

—*Innocents Abroad,* 1869, ch. 61
(describing the highly touted *Quaker City* excursion)

Go, and reform—or, mark my words—some day, for your sins, you will die and go to hell or Hadleyburg—TRY AND MAKE IT THE FORMER.

—"The Man That Corrupted Hadleyburg," story, 1899

Go and surprise the whole country by doing something right.

—"Open Letter to Commodore Vanderbilt," 1869

INSURANCE

When he moved to Hartford, Connecticut, which was the insurance capital of the country, Mark Twain bought stock in an insurance company, and it changed his life, or at least his attitude toward life.

"Ever since I have been a director in an accident-insurance company I have felt that I am a better man. Life has seemed more precious. Accidents have assumed a kindlier aspect. Distressing special providences have lost half their horror. I look upon a cripple now with affectionate interest—as an advertisement. I do not seem to care for poetry any more. I do not care for politics—even agriculture does not excite me. But to me now there is a charm about a railway collision that is unspeakable."

This is a poor old ship, and ought to be insured and sunk.

Following the Equator, 1897, vol. 2, ch. 2

INTELLIGENCE

He fairly oozes intelligence.

—*New York Times*, 1900
(about a reader who confessed to
having read all Mark Twain's works)

A man's intellect is stored powder; it cannot touch itself off; the fire must come from the outside.

—*Notebook*, 1898

There isn't any way to libel the intelligence of the human race.

—"Theodore Roosevelt," in DeVoto,
Mark Twain in Eruption, 1940

INTEREST

A great and priceless thing is a new interest! How it takes possession of a man! how it clings to him, how it rides him!

—*A Tramp Abroad*, 1880, vol. 2, ch. 6

We take a natural interest in novelties, but it is against nature to take an interest in familiar things.

—*Following the Equator*, 1897, vol. 1, ch. 18

INTERVIEWS

When Mark Twain was living in Vienna in 1897, a reporter from the *New York Times* came for an interview. When the man arrived, Mark Twain was writing in bed, which was his custom. "Show him up, Livy!" he called to his wife.

Mrs. Clemens said, "Youth, don't you think it will be a little uncomfortable for him, your being in bed?"

"Why, Livy, if you think so," Mark Twain replied genially, "have the other bed made up for him."

INTERRUPTIONS

Mark Twain was a connoisseur of the fine art of storytelling, and he had definite ideas about how it should and should not be done. Few things irked him more than storytellers who interrupted themselves to ask if the listener had heard the story before.

He recalled an encounter with the actor Henry Irving, who asked him if he had heard a certain story. Twain said politely, "No." Irving launched into the story and then interrupted it to ask, "Are you sure you haven't heard this before?" Twain again replied that he had not.

Irving continued the story to the climax and then paused again to ask if Twain had heard it before. Twain replied, "I can lie once, I can lie twice for courtesy's sake, but I cannot lie three times. I not only heard the story, I wrote it."

INTRODUCTIONS

Early in his career as a lecturer, Mark Twain grew so vexed with the bumbling introductions he received from local leaders that he resolved to do away with formal introductions altogether and introduce himself.

One of the introductions he received which settled him on this policy came from a miner who was nominated to introduce Mark Twain to a Nevada audience. The miner, who was unaccustomed to public speaking, introduced Twain with these words:

"I don't know anything about this man. Anyhow, I only know two things about him. One is, he has never been in jail. And the other is, I don't know why."

INVENTIONS

Mark Twain always had a weakness for new inventions; he was fascinated by them, and over the years he lost more than half a million dollars investing in various contraptions—including the Paige typesetter—which did not pan out. Once, after a series of bad investments had temporarily tempered his enthusiasm for technology, he was approached by a tall, awkward young man with a mysterious device under his arm.

Mark Twain listened politely to what the young man had to

say, but explained that he had been burnt once too often and was not interested.

"But I'm not asking you to invest a fortune," said the young man. "You can have as large a share as you want to for $500."

The author shook his head and the tall, stooped figure started away. Mark Twain, saddened by the sight of this pathetic young man, called after him. "What did you say your name was again?"

"Bell," was the reply. "Alexander Graham Bell."

The first thing you want in a new country is a patent office. . . . A country without a patent office and good patent laws was just a crab, and couldn't travel any way but sideways or backwards.

—*A Connecticut Yankee*, 1889, ch. 9

INVENTORS

Mark Twain was an inventor in his own right. He invented a scrapbook, called Mark Twain's Scrapbook, "the only rational scrapbook the world has ever seen." It was patented in 1871 and earned more money than his books that year.

In his notebooks, Mark Twain recorded ideas for some inventions that would later prove to be quite practical. In 1885, he conceived of the idea of microfilm, an invention that did not come into actual use until the First World War. In 1888, he made notes about an invention that he believed would eventually be ubiquitous. It would utilize "pictures transferred by light," similar to modern television. In his novel *Pudd'nhead Wilson*, published in 1894, the plot hinges on the use of fingerprinting, which was a revolutionary idea at the time, but now is standard.

Mark Twain called inventors "the creators of the world—after God." But invariably, whenever he invested in the inventions of others he lost money. Eventually he became bitter about it. In his old age he received a letter from an author who had written a book to assist inventors and patentees. Mark Twain's reply:

Dear Sir: I have, as you say, been interested in patents and patentees. If your book tells how to exterminate inventors, send me nine editions. Send them by express.

S. L. Clemens

IRISH

Give an Irishman lager for a month, and he's a dead man. An Irishman is lined with copper, and the beer corrodes it. But whisky polishes the copper and is the saving of him.

—*Life on the Mississippi,* 1883, ch. 23

IRREVERENCE

When a thing is sacred to me it is impossible for me to be irreverent toward it. I cannot call to mind a single instance where I have ever been irreverent, except toward the things which were sacred to other people.

—"Is Shakespeare Dead?" essay, 1909

True irreverence is disrespect for another man's god.

—*Following the Equator,* 1897, vol. 2, ch. 17

Irreverence is the champion of liberty and its only sure defense.

—Notebook, 1888

ITALY

The Creator made Italy with designs by Michelangelo.

—*Innocents Abroad,* 1869, ch. 27

Medicis are good enough for Florence. Let her plant Medicis and build grand monuments over them to testify how gratefully she was wont to lick the hand that scourged her.

—*Innocents Abroad,* 1869, ch. 24

JAMES, HENRY

One of Mark Twain's least favorite writers was Henry James. Perhaps Mark Twain could not forgive James for forsaking America to become a British citizen. Whatever the reason, Twain rebuffed most attempts to persuade him to read James. Once, when William Dean Howells recommended *The Bostonians,* Mark Twain replied, "I would rather be damned to John Bunyan's heaven than read that."

JOHNS HOPKINS

In 1888, Mark Twain offered some free advice to the administration of Johns Hopkins University in Baltimore. "I told them I believed they were perfectly competent to run a college, as far as the higher branches of education are concerned, but what they needed was a little help here and there from a practical commercial mind. I said the public are sensitive to little things, and they wouldn't ever have full confidence in a college that didn't know how to spell John."

JOKES

I tried him with mild jokes, then with severe ones.

—"A Deception," sketch, 1872

The only way to classify the majestic ages of some of those jokes was by geologic periods.

—*A Connecticut Yankee,* 1889, ch. 4

JOAN OF ARC

She was the Genius of Patriotism—she was Patriotism embodied, concreted, made flesh.

—*Joan of Arc,* 1896, conclusion

She is easily and by far the most extraordinary person the human race has ever produced.

—"Saint Joan of Arc," essay, 1904

JOURNALISM

Mark Twain served in various editorial positions before he retired at forty to become a full-time free-lance writer. One of the reasons he retired was that he found journalism too strenuous. His experience in Tennessee, as described in the semiautobiographical story "Journalism in Tennessee," was particularly discouraging. The editor in chief of the Tennessee newspaper complained that Mark Twain's writing was too insipid and insisted on rewriting it to make it more thoroughly libelous.

> While he was in the midst of his work, somebody shot at him through the open window, and marred the symmetry of my ear.
> "Ah," said he, "that is that scoundrel Smith, of the *Moral Volcano*—he was due yesterday." And he snatched a navy revolver from his belt and fired. Smith dropped, shot in the thigh. The shot spoiled Smith's aim, who was just taking a

second chance, and he crippled a stranger. It was me. Merely a finger shot off.

Then the chief editor went on with his erasures and interlineations. Just as he finished them a hand-grenade came down the stove-pipe, and the explosion shivered the stove into a thousand fragments. However, it did no further damage, except that a vagrant piece knocked a couple of my teeth out.

"That stove is utterly ruined," said the chief editor.

After a series of similar disruptions during his first day on the job, Mark Twain decided to retire from his editorial position and seek a safer line of work. He concluded, "Tennessean journalism is too stirring for me."

JOY

Grief can take care of itself; but to get the full value of a joy you must have somebody to divide it with.

—*Following the Equator*, 1897, vol. 2, ch. 12

JURY

We have a criminal jury system which is superior to any in the world; and its efficiency is only marred by the difficulty of finding twelve men every day who don't know anything and can't read.

—Fourth of July speech, 1873

JUSTICE

In this world the real penalty, the sharp one, the lasting one, never falls otherwise than on the wrong person.

—Neider, *Autobiography*, 1959, ch. 39

The rain . . . falls upon the just and the unjust alike; a thing which would not happen if I were superintending the rain's affairs. No, I would rain softly and sweetly on the just, but if I caught a sample of the unjust outdoors I would drown him.

—Paine, *Mark Twain: A Biography*, 1912, vol. 3, p. 1440

KINGS

Kings is kings, and you got to make allowances. Take them all around, they're a mighty ornery lot. It's the way they're raised.

—*Huckleberry Finn*, 1884, ch. 23

Those transparent swindles, transmissible nobility and kingship.

—*A Connecticut Yankee*, 1889, ch. 28

Kings should go to school to their own laws at times, and so learn mercy.

—*The Prince and the Pauper*, 1882, ch. 27

"We hold these truths to be self-evident: that all monarchs are usurpers, and descendants of usurpers, for the reason that no throne was ever set up in this world by the will, freely exercised, of the only body possessing the legitimate right to set it up—the numerical mass of the nation."

—Letter to Sylvester Baxter, 1889

KIPLING, RUDYARD

When Rudyard Kipling, still a young man of twenty-four, came to America in 1889, he made a pilgrimage to Elmira, New York, to meet Mark Twain, whom he considered the greatest writer America had ever produced. At the time, Mark Twain had never heard of Rudyard Kipling. "In those days you could have carried Kipling around in a lunchbasket," Twain recalled, "but now he fills the world." The two men had a genial chat, which Kipling later described rapturously.

"I have seen Mark Twain this golden morning," he exulted, "have shaken his hand and smoked a cigar—no, two cigars—with him, and talked with him for more than two hours! . . . Reading his books, I had striven to get an idea of his personality, and all my preconceived notions were wrong and beneath the reality. Blessed is the man who finds no disillusion when he is brought face to face with a revered writer."

After Kipling departed, Mrs. Clemens asked what her husband thought of the young writer. Mark Twain replied that he thought this strange visitor from India was the most remarkable man he had ever met: "Between us, we cover all knowledge; he knows all that can be known, and I know the rest."

KNOWLEDGE

The less a man knows the bigger the noise he makes and the higher the salary he commands.

—"How I Edited an Agricultural
Paper," story, 1870

Each of us knows it all, and knows he knows it all—the rest, to a man, are fools and deluded. One man knows there is a hell, the next one knows there isn't; one man knows monarchy is best, the next one knows it isn't; one man knows high tariff is right, the next man knows it isn't; one age knows there are

131

witches, the next one knows there aren't; one sect knows its religion is the only true one, there are sixty-four thousand five hundred million sects that know it isn't so.

—"3,000 Years Among the Microbes,"
story, 1905

You may have noticed that the less I know about a subject the more confidence I have, and the more new light I throw on it.

—Johnson, *A Bibliography of Mark Twain,* 1935, p. 165

I have told him all I know about it. And now he knows nothing about it himself.

—"The Begum of Bengal," speech,
1907

LABOR

Who are the oppressed? The many: the nations of the earth; the valuable personages; the workers.

—"Knights of Labor, the New Dynasty," speech, 1886

LANGUAGE

What is the real function, the essential function, the supreme function of language? Isn't it merely to convey ideas and emotions?

—"Simplified Spelling," speech, 1906

I have a prejudice against people who print things in a foreign language and add no translation. When I am the reader, and the other considers me able to do the translating myself, he pays me quite a nice compliment—but if he would do the translating for me I would try to get along without the compliment.

—A Tramp Abroad, 1880, vol. 1, ch. 16

LATE

Mark Twain once arrived over an hour late for a lecture in Duluth, Minnesota. Although the delay was not his fault, the crowd was impatient and somewhat irascible by the time he showed up. But Mark Twain disarmed them by strolling into the lecture hall in a leisurely fashion and saying, "I am glad that my strenuous efforts did succeed in getting me here just in time."

The crowd laughed and their hostility melted away.

LAUGHTER

Your race, in its poverty, has unquestionably one really effective weapon—laughter. Power, money, persuasion, supplication, persecution—these can lift at a colossal humbug—push it a little—weaken it a little, century by century; but only laughter can blow it to rags and atoms at a blast. Against the assault of laughter nothing can stand.

—"The Mysterious Stranger," story, 1916, ch. 10

Such a laugh was money in a man's pocket, because it cut down on the doctor's bills like everything.

—Tom Sawyer, 1876, ch. 30

LAW

To succeed in the other trades, capacity must be shown; in the law, concealment of it will do.

—Following the Equator, 1897, vol. 2, ch. 1

Trial by jury is the palladium of our liberties. I do not know what a palladium is, having never seen a palladium, but it is a good thing no doubt at any rate.

—Roughing It, 1872, ch. 49

We have an insanity plea that would have saved Cain.

—Fourth of July speech, 1873

There is no end to the laws, and no beginning to the execution of them.

—"Temperance and Women's Rights," essay, 1923

The departmental interpreters of the laws in Washington . . . can always be depended on to take any reasonably good law and interpret the common sense all out of it.

—Letter to H. C. Christiancy, December 18, 1887

It would not be possible for Noah to do in our day what he was permitted to do in his own. . . . The inspector would come and examine the Ark, and make all sorts of objections.

—"About All Kinds of Ships," essay, 1892

LAWSUIT

Mark Twain was one of the most litigious writers in literary history. He filed a number of lawsuits against publishers and others who he believed were trying to cheat him. But he had little luck in the courts, and eventually these lawsuits drained his financial and spiritual resources. It was with an element of self-mockery that he wrote to a friend:

"I can't do no literary work the rest of this year because I'm meditating another lawsuit and looking around for a defendant."

LAWYER

Mark Twain had just finished addressing a New England society banquet when the attorney William M. Evarts stood up with his hands in his pockets, as was his custom, and remarked: "Does it not seem unusual to this gathering that a professional humorist should really appear funny?"

Twain arose and responded in his habitual drawl: "Does it not also appear strange to this assembly that a lawyer should have his hands in his own pockets?"

They all laid their heads together like as many lawyers when they are gettin' ready to prove that a man's heirs ain't got any right to his property.

—Lorch, *Iowa Journal of History and Politics,* July 1929

LAZINESS

I am no lazier now than I was forty years ago, but that is because I reached the limit forty years ago. You can't go beyond possibility.

—Neider, *Autobiography,* 1959, ch. 23

LEADERSHIP

A statesman gains little by the arbitrary exercise of ironclad authority upon all occasions that offer, for this wounds the just pride of his subordinates, and thus tends to undermine his strength. A little concession, now and then, where it can do no harm, is the wiser policy.

—*A Connecticut Yankee,* 1889, ch. 16

LEARNING

Never learn to do anything: if you don't learn, you'll always find someone else to do it for you.

—Wagenknecht, *Mark Twain, the Man and His Work,* 1935, p. 10

Now let that teach you a lesson—I don't know just what it is.

—"Memories," speech, 1906

LECTURE

Mark Twain often recalled his first lecture, in 1866 in San Francisco. "I had sold two hundred tickets among my personal friends, but I feared they might not come," he wrote in *Roughing It.* To ensure his success, he asked a couple of pals to sit in prominent positions in the audience. He asked them not to "investigate" his jokes but to respond immediately, thereby cuing the audience when to laugh. Then Twain found one gentleman with a laugh that was "hung on a hair trigger" and he placed this confederate in a strategic location in the front-center section of the theater. A glance from Mark Twain was agreed upon as the signal to begin laughing.

The plan worked admirably well and before long the house was roaring with laughter. "Inferior jokes never fared so royally before," said Twain. "Presently I delivered a bit of serious matter with impressive unction (it was my pet), and the audience listened with an absorbed hush that gratified me more than any applause." But as he finished this poetic passage, he glanced up at the fellow with the hair-trigger laugh. That touched off an explosion of laughter.

"My poor little morsel of pathos was ruined," lamented Mark Twain. "It was taken in good faith as an intentional joke, and the prize one of the entertainment, and I wisely let it go at that."

There's a great moral difference between a lecture and a speech— for when you deliver a lecture you get good pay, but when you make a speech you don't get a cent.

—Republican rally speech, 1880

Lecturing is gymnastics, chest-expander, medicine, mind-healer, blues-destroyer, all in one.

—Pond, *The Eccentricities of Genius,* 1900, p. 225

LECTURE CIRCUIT

When Mark Twain was on the lecture circuit, he was sometimes scheduled to appear in the same town twice in the same season. On one such occasion, he prefaced his second appearance with this published appeal to the public:

"All who have not already heard the lecture can pay a dollar and come in; and all who have heard it before can commute for two dollars apiece and remain at home if they prefer. In which case the police will be instructed not to disturb them."

LECTURERS

One time, Mark Twain arrived in town just before he was scheduled to lecture. Finding no reception committee, he walked straight to the lecture hall, where the crowd was gathering. As he tried to press through, he was stopped cold by the ticket-taker.

Said Twain: "It's all right, I am the lecturer."

The ticket-taker shook his head. "No you don't," he chuckled. "Three of you have got in so far, but the next lecturer that goes in tonight *pays.*"

Mark Twain paid.

LEGENDS

Sometimes it is a fine line between a legend and a lie. When Mark Twain was a young man, he once met an old man who claimed to have crossed the Delaware River with George Washington.

"Were you also with Washington when he took that hack at the cherry tree?" a skeptical Mark Twain asked the old man, smiling.

The old man, who had apparently never heard of the legend of the cherry tree, hesitated for a few moments. Then he said, "Of course I was there. I was with George Washington when it happened. In fact, I drove that hack myself!"

LIARS

On a nostalgic trip up the Mississippi, Mark Twain stopped at a tavern, where he was accosted in the sitting room by an eager young man.

"Mr. Clemens, I am a newspaper reporter and have been commissioned to ask you a few questions," said the young man. "What is humor?"

"Humor is the good-natured side of a truth," answered Twain.

"What are the past and the future?"

"For the majority of us, the past is a regret, the future an experiment."

"What is man's most universal weakness?"
"Lying."

The young man arose. "Sir, you inspire me to tell the truth. I am not a reporter. It was a deception just to meet you."

Mark Twain grinned. "A man is never more truthful than when he acknowledges himself a liar. I am glad to meet you, sir. Wait a moment. When I say that, I am a liar, too. And now let two liars shake hands."

LIBERTY

Irreverence is the champion of liberty.

—Notebook, 1888

LIES

Never waste a lie; you never know when you may need it.

—Henderson, *Mark Twain,* 1912, p. 189

The history of our race, and each individual's experience, are sown thick with evidence that a truth is not hard to kill and that a lie told well is immortal.

—"Advice to Youth," speech, 1882

Carlyle said "a lie cannot live." It shows that he did not know how to tell them.

—Neider, *Autobiography,* 1959, ch. 11

Why will you humbug yourselves with that foolish notion that no lie is a lie except a spoken one?

—"Was It Heaven? Or Hell?" story, 1902

Never tell a lie—except for practice.

—Henderson, *Mark Twain,* 1912, p. 188

A lie can travel halfway around the world while the truth is putting on its shoes.

—Attributed

LIFE

Someone once asked Mark Twain if he thought life was worth living. Twain responded: "A man once wrote to the editor of London *Punch* and asked, 'Is life worth living?' Then came the answer, now known all over the world—'It depends upon the liver.' But that does not embrace the whole of the human family. Ask the question of a cynic and he will not say that life depends on the liver but the gall bladder."

Oh Death where is thy sting! It has none. But life has.

—Notebook, 1894

He had arrived at that point where presently the illusions would cease and he would have entered upon the realities of life, and God help the man that has arrived at that point.

—"Jack Van Nostrand," speech, 1905

Only he who has seen better days and lives to see better days again knows their full value.

—Notebook, 1902

There was never yet an uninteresting life. Such a thing is an impossibility. Inside of the dullest exterior there is a drama, a comedy, and a tragedy.

—"The Refuge of the Derelicts,"
story, 1905

LIGHTNING

Thunder is good, thunder is impressive; but it is lightning that does the work.

—Letter dated August 28, 1908

The trouble isn't that there are too many fools, but that the lightning isn't distributed right.

—Johnson, *More Maxims of Mark*, 1927, p. 13

LIKING

He liked to like people, therefore people liked him.

—*Joan of Arc*, 1896, bk. 2, ch. 16

He made me like him. . . . He made me better satisfied with myself than I had ever been before.

—*Following the Equator*, 1897, vol. 1, ch. 25

LINCOLN, ABRAHAM

Mark Twain visited Lincoln's house in Springfield, Illinois, with Congressman Billy Mason.

"What a pity it was that fate did not intend that Lincoln should marry Ann Rutledge," remarked Mason. "It seems that fate governs our lives and plans history in advance."

"Yes," Mark Twain mused. "Had Lincoln married the dear one of his heart's love he might have led a happy but obscure life and the world would never have heard of him. Happiness seeks obscurity to enjoy itself. A good-looking milkmaid might have kept Alexander the Great from conquering the world."

"Well, doesn't that prove that what is to be will be?" asked Mason.

Mark Twain shook his head. "The only thing it proves is that what has been was."

LITERATURE

Persons attempting to find a motive in this narrative will be prosecuted; persons attempting to find a moral in it will be banished; persons attempting to find a plot in it will be shot.

—*Huckleberry Finn*, 1884, preface

Read it aloud. I may be wrong, still it is my conviction that one cannot get out of finely wrought literature all that is in it by reading it mutely.

—"William Dean Howells," essay, 1906

Creed and opinion change with time, and their symbols perish; but Literature and its temples are sacred to all creeds and inviolate.

—Letter to Millicent Library,
Fairhaven, Massachusetts, 1894

They always talk handsomely about the literature of the land. . . . And in the midst of their enthusiasm they turn around and do what they can to discourage it.

—Speech in Congress on copyright,
1906

No man has an appreciation so various that his judgment is good upon all varieties of literary work.

—Clara Clemens, *My Father, Mark Twain*, 1931, p. 47

To my mind that literature is best and most enduring which is characterized by a noble simplicity.

—"Visit to Canada," speech, 1881

My works are like water. The works of the great masters are like wine. But everyone drinks water.

—Notebook, 1885

LONELINESS

I feel for Adam and Eve now, for I know how it was with them. . . . The Garden of Eden I now know was an unendurable solitude. I know that the advent of the serpent was a welcome change—anything for society.

—Paine, *Mark Twain: A Biography*, 1912, vol. 3, p. 1315

LOQUACITY

Mark Twain was a silent participant at a dinner party in Hartford one evening. When he was chided afterward for not saying anything, he replied that the host had talked so incessantly as to leave little opportunity.

"It reminds me of the man who was reproached by a friend, who said, 'I think it a shame that you have not spoken to your wife for fifteen years. How do you justify it?"

"And the husband answered: 'I didn't want to interrupt her.' "

LOVE

"The fresh-crowned hero fell without firing a shot." It is love at first sight for Tom Sawyer that electrifying instant when he first spots Becky Thatcher. And new love leaves little room for old love. "A certain Amy Lawrence vanished out of his heart and left not even a memory of herself behind. He thought he had loved her to distraction, he had regarded his passion as adoration; and behold it was only a poor little evanescent partiality."

Love leads to talk and talk leads to love. Ultimately, Tom and Becky exchange lovers' vows by the banks of the sacred river. "No, I'll never love anybody but you, Tom," says Becky passionately, "and I'll never marry anybody but you—and you ain't to marry anybody but me, either."

This is young love, simple and uncomplicated. A more mature sexual love is described by Mark Twain in *Eve's Diary* (1906), after the Fall, when Eve reconciles herself to her fate as woman and mate. "The Garden is lost, but I have found *him,* and am content," she writes. "If I ask myself why I love him, I find I do not know, and do not really much care to know; so I suppose that this kind of love is not a product of reasonings and statistics." Shedding her romantic illusions about Adam one by one, she comes to a strange and simple conclusion: "Then, why is it that I love him? *Merely because he is masculine,* I think. . . . Yes, I think I love him merely because he is *mine* and is *masculine.*" Eve's final conclusion about love is Mark Twain's conclusion: "Love is not a product of reasonings and statistics. It just *comes*—none knows whence—and cannot explain itself."

Love is a madness; if thwarted it develops fast.

—"The Memorable Assassination," essay, 1917

I wanted an idol, and I wanted to be my idol's idol; nothing less than mutual idolatry would satisfy my fervent nature.

—"The Esquimau Maiden's
Romance," story, 1893

The frankest and freest product of the human mind and heart is a love letter; the writer gets his limitless freedom of statement and expression from his sense that no stranger is going to see what he is writing.

—Neider, Autobiography, 1959, preface

When you fish for love, bait with your heart, not your brain.

—Notebook, 1898

LYING

When Mark Twain returned to America in October 1900, with all his debts paid after nine years of exile, he was met by reporters, who came aboard the ship and interviewed him while he was lounging in a deck chair.

"Some people lie when they tell the truth," said Mark Twain. "I tell the truth lying."

MADNESS

Of course, no man is entirely in his right mind at any time.

—"The Mysterious Stranger," story,
1916, ch. 10

MAJORITY

Whenever you find you are on the side of the majority, it is time to pause and reflect.

—Notebook, 1904

MAN

Man is the only animal that blushes. Or needs to.

—*Following the Equator*, 1897, vol. 1, ch. 27

Man was made at the end of the week's work, when God was tired.

—Notebook, 1903

Man is the Religious Animal. He is the only Religious Animal. He is the only animal that has the True Religion—several of them.

—"The Lowest Animal," essay, 1897

MANNERS

Mark Twain's butler George was a man who was hired one day to wash the windows and ended up staying for eighteen years. His manners were almost perfect, but not quite.

"When George first came to us he was one of the most religious of men," wrote Mark Twain. "He had but one fault—young George Washington's. But I have trained him; and now it fairly breaks Mrs. Clemens's heart to hear him stand at that front door and lie to an unwelcome visitor."

Good breeding consists in concealing how much we think of ourselves and how little we think of the other person.

—Notebook, 1898

Truth is good manners; manners are a fiction.

—"The Mysterious Stranger," story, 1916, ch. 3

No real gentleman will tell the naked truth in the presence of the ladies.

—"A Double-Barreled Detective Story," story, 1902

The highest perfection of politeness is only a beautiful edifice, built, from the base to the dome, of graceful and gilded forms of charitable and unselfish lying.

—"On the Decay of the Art of Lying," speech, 1880

MARRIAGE

People talk about beautiful friendships between two persons of the same sex. What is the best of that sort, as compared with the friendship of man and wife, where the best impulses and highest ideals of both are the same? There is no place for comparison between the two friendships; the one is earthly, the other divine.

—*A Connecticut Yankee,* 1889, ch. 41

Love seems the swiftest, but it is the slowest of all growths. No man or woman really knows what perfect love is until they have been married a quarter of a century.

—Notebook, 1894

Both marriage and death ought to be welcome: the one promises happiness, doubtless the other assures it.

—Letter to Will Bowen, November 4, 1888

MASSES

The master minds of all nations, in all ages, have sprung in affluent multitude from the mass of the nations, and from the mass of the nation only—not from its privileged classes.

—*A Connecticut Yankee,* 1889, ch. 25

MASTURBATION

Of all the various kinds of sexual intercourse this has least to recommend it. As an amusement it is too fleeting. As an occupation it is too wearing. As a public exhibition, there is no money in it.

—"The Science of Onanism," speech, 1879

MAXIM

The proper proportions of a maxim: a minimum of sound to a maximum of sense.

—Holograph, December 12, 1897

ME

The question of who or what the Me is, is not a simple one at all.

—"What Is Man?" essay, 1906

MEDICINE

In a speech to a group of physicians, Mark Twain declared that the art of diagnosis was what distinguished the modern man of medicine from the old medicine man. He announced that he had himself joined the medical fraternity, taking up practice in a small town in Connecticut where there were only four doctors. One day a sailor walked into town, "with a rolling gait and a distressed face. We asked him what was the matter. We always hold consultations on every case, as there isn't enough business for four. He said he didn't know, but that he was a sailor, and perhaps that might help us to give a diagnosis. We treated him for that, and I never saw a man die more peacefully."

MELANCHOLY

Everybody was sorry she died. . . . But I reckoned that with her disposition she was having a better time in the graveyard.

—*Huckleberry Finn,* 1884, ch. 17 (of Emmeline Grangerford)

MEMORY

Mark Twain spoke at a New York dinner given by Andrew Carnegie for Sidney Lee on March 28, 1903. During his speech, Twain casually referred to the time when he had loaned Carnegie a million dollars.

Carnegie promptly piped up: "That had slipped my memory!"

Mark Twain paused, looked dourly down at Carnegie from the podium and said, "Then, the next time I'll take a receipt."

My memory was never loaded with anything but blank cartridges.

—*Life on the Mississippi,* 1883, ch. 6

The natural way provided by nature and the construction of the human mind for the discovery of a forgotten event is to employ another forgotten event for its resurrection.

—Neider, *Autobiography*, 1959, ch. 29

Astonishing things can be done with the human memory if you will devote it faithfully to one particular line of business.

—*Life on the Mississippi*, 1883, ch. 13

It isn't so astonishing, the number of things that I can remember, as the number of things I can remember that aren't so.

—Paine, *Mark Twain: A Biography*, 1912, vol. 3, p. 1269

MENTAL TELEPATHY

For many years, Mark Twain withheld the publication of "Mental Telegraphy"—an essay that described numerous instances of thought transference from his own personal life—because he "feared that the public would treat the thing as a joke and throw it aside, whereas I was in earnest."

Although Twain was a skeptic in religious matters, he was a lifelong believer in mental telepathy and certain other psychic phenomena. "Certainly mental telegraphy is an industry which is always silently at work—oftener than otherwise, perhaps, when we are not suspecting that it is affecting our thought."

I once made a great discovery . . . that certain sorts of things which, from the beginning of the world, had always been regarded as merely "curious coincidences"—that is to say, accidents—were no more accidental than is the sending and receiving of a telegram an accident. I made this discovery sixteen or seventeen years ago, and gave it a name—"Mental Telegraphy."

—"Mental Telegraphy," essay, 1891

MICHELANGELO

On his first visit to Rome, Mark Twain was deeply impressed by the works of Michelangelo, but he gradually got tired of having Michelangelo thrown up to him all the time.

"I do not want Michael Angelo for breakfast—for luncheon—for tea—for supper—for between meals," he complained.

"In Florence, he painted everything, designed everything, nearly, and what he did not design he used to sit on a favorite stone and look at, and they showed us the stone.

"He designed St. Peter's; he designed the Pope; he designed the Pantheon, the uniform of the Pope's soldiers, the Tiber, the Vatican . . . the eternal bore designed the Eternal City. . . .

"Lump the whole thing! Say that the Creator made Italy from designs by Michelangelo!" This ejaculation was aimed at a guide who mentioned Michelangelo's name one too many times.

Pudd'nhead Wilson's Calendar offers Twain's final word on Michelangelo. "Even popularity can be overdone. In Rome, along at first, you are full of regrets that Michelangelo died; but by and by you only regret that you didn't see him do it."

MIRACLE

There is nothing more awe-inspiring than a miracle except the credulity that can take it at par.

—Notebook, 1904

MISERY

The *sum* of wrong and misery shall always keep exact step with the *sum* of human blessedness.

—Paine, *Mark Twain: A Biography*,
1912, vol. 3, p. 1469

MISSING PERSONS

In May 1907, Mark Twain was aboard the yacht of his friend Henry Rogers when it sailed from Hampton Roads, Virginia, in a heavy fog. For a few days there were rumors in Virginia that the yacht had disappeared at sea. When Mark Twain heard about the rumors, he issued a statement, which appeared in the *New York Times:*

TWAIN AND YACHT DISAPPEAR AT SEA
MARK TWAIN INVESTIGATING

You can assure my Virginia friends that I will make an exhaustive investigation of this report that I have been lost at

sea. If there is any foundation for the report, I will at once
apprise the anxious public. I sincerely hope there is no foundation for the report, and I also hope that judgment will be
suspended until I ascertain the true state of affairs.

MISSIONARIES

O kind missionary, O compassionate missionary, leave China!
Come home and convert these Christians!

—"The United States of
Lyncherdom," essay, 1923

We are all missionaries (propagandists of our views). Each of us
disapproves of the other missionaries.

—Notebook, 1905

MISSISSIPPI

Mark Twain and some rivermen were sitting around swapping
stories about the Mississippi and how high its banks had risen at
floodtide.

Each man was trying to outdo the others. Jake Anders said he
had seen it fifty miles wide at Natchez. Billy Sharp said some tall
pines on top of a hill on his property bore the high-water marks
on their topmost boughs.

Mark Twain listened patiently to each man's boast, then
cleared his throat. "Gentlemen, you don't know what a wide river
is. I've seen this river so wide that it had only one bank."

The face of the water, in time, became a wonderful book—a book
that was a dead language to the uneducated passenger, but which
told its mind to me without reserve, delivering its most cherished
secrets as clearly as if it uttered them with a voice. And it was not
a book to be read once and thrown aside, for it had a new story
to tell every day.

—*Life on the Mississippi*, 1883, ch. 9

MOB

The pitifulest thing out is a mob; that's what an army is—a mob; they don't fight with courage that's born in them, but with courage that's borrowed from their mass, and from their officers. But a mob without any man at the head of it, is *beneath* pitifulness.

—*Huckleberry Finn*, 1884, ch. 22

MODESTY

The man who is ostentatious of his modesty is twin to the statue that wears the fig-leaf.

—*Following the Equator*, 1897, vol. 2, ch. 14

I was born modest; not all over, but in spots.

—*A Connecticut Yankee*, 1889, ch. 16

He . . . made the most of his wound, and went swaggering around in his bandages showing off like an innocent big child. . . . He was prouder of being wounded than a really modest person would be of being killed.

—*Joan of Arc*, 1896, bk. 2, ch. 27

MONARCHY

Mark Twain was opposed to any form of monarchy, even constitutional monarchies with royal figureheads. He proposed that chimpanzees be substituted for the British royal family. "A royal family of chimpanzees would answer every purpose, be worshipped as abjectly by the nation, and be cheaper."

A monarch when good is entitled to the consideration which we accord to a pirate who keeps Sunday School between crimes; when bad he is entitled to none at all.

—Notebook, 1888

MONEY

Mark Twain was of two minds about money. In his life he made a fortune and he lost a fortune, more than once. He was born in poverty, he was wealthy at the age of fifty, bankrupt at sixty, and wealthy again at seventy. His life story was a story of rags to riches, yet there was always a part of him, like Huckleberry Finn, more comfortable in rags.

Mark Twain gave a name to the materialistic age he lived in: "The Gilded Age." He savagely satirized plutocrats in print. Yet one of his best friends, Henry Rogers, was a millionaire.

Once when Mark Twain was in Bermuda on a vacation with Rogers, a Bermudian remarked to Twain, "Your friend Rogers is a good fellow. It's a pity his money is tainted."

"It's twice tainted," said Twain, nodding knowingly. "Tain't yours, and tain't mine."

The lack of money is the root of all evil.

—Johnson, *More Maxims of Mark*, 1927,
p. 10

God was left out of the Constitution but was furnished a front seat on the coins of the country.

—"Andrew Carnegie," in DeVoto,
Mark Twain in Eruption, 1940

The motto ["In God We Trust"] stated a lie. If this nation has ever trusted in God, that time has gone by, for nearly half a century almost its entire trust has been in the Republican party and the dollar—mainly the dollar.

—"Andrew Carnegie," in DeVoto,
Mark Twain in Eruption, 1940

There was never a nation in the world that put its whole trust in God. . . . I think it would better read, "Within certain judicious limitations we trust in God," and if there isn't enough room on the coin for this, why, enlarge the coin.

—"Jumping to Conclusions," speech,
1908

Some men worship rank, some worship heroes, some worship God, and over these ideals they dispute—but they all worship money.

—Notebook, 1898

Make money and the whole world will conspire to call you a gentleman.

—Attributed

Simple rules for saving money: To save half, when you are fired by an eager impulse to contribute to charity, wait and count forty. To save three-quarters, count sixty. To save it all, count sixty-five.

—Following the Equator, 1897, vol. 2, ch. 11

MORALS

Mark Twain often described himself as a "professional moralist." In a speech in London in June 1899, he told of the turning point in his moral development. It was one day in his youth when he stole a watermelon out of a farmer's wagon while the farmer was waiting on another customer: " 'stole' is a harsh term, I withdrew—I retired that watermelon—and I retired with it." Much to his chagrin, the watermelon turned out to be unripe.

"The minute I saw it was green I was sorry, and began to reflect—reflection is the beginning of reform. . . . I said to myself: 'What ought a boy to do who has stolen a green watermelon? What would George Washington do, the father of his country, the only American who could not tell a lie? What would he do? There is only one right, high, noble thing for any boy to do who has stolen a watermelon of that class; he must make restitution; he must restore that stolen property to its rightful owner.' I said I would do it when I made that good resolution. I felt it would be a noble, uplifting obligation. I rose up spiritually stronger and refreshed. I carried that watermelon back—what was left of it— and restored it to the farmer, and made him give me a ripe one in its place."

Always do right. This will gratify some people, and astonish the rest.

—Note to the Young People's Society, 1901

The Moral Sense teaches us what is right, and how to avoid it—when unpopular.

—"The United States of Lyncherdom," essay, 1923

No brute ever does a cruel thing—that is the monopoly of those with the Moral Sense.

—"The Mysterious Stranger," story,
1916, ch. 5

Morals are of inestimable value, for every man is born crammed with sin microbes, and the only thing that can extirpate these sin microbes is morals.

—Seventieth-birthday speech, 1905

Morals are an acquirement—like music, like a foreign language, like piety, poker, paralysis—no man is born with them.

—Seventieth-birthday speech, 1905

A man should not be without morals; it is better to have bad morals than none at all.

—Notebook, 1894

I have lived a severely moral life. But it would be a mistake for other people to try that, or for me to recommend it. Very few would succeed: you have to have a perfectly colossal stock of morals.

—Seventieth-birthday speech, 1905

It is not best that we use our morals week days; it gets them out of repair for Sundays.

—Notebook, 1898

MOSES

In *Roughing It*, Mark Twain mentions the legendary stage-driver Ben Holliday in an anecdote about a nineteen-year-old New Yorker who had never heard of Moses.

After Twain patiently explained about the great leader who guided the children of Israel for forty years across a desolate desert three hundred miles wide, the brash young man was utterly unimpressed:

"Forty years? Only three hundred miles? Humph! Ben Holliday would have fetched them through in thirty-six hours!"

MOSQUITOES

There are some regional rivalries of long standing in the western states about the size of their respective mosquitoes. Most other states contend that the Arkansas mosquito is the prince of mosquitoes. But Arkansans deny it.

Mark Twain records in *Life on the Mississippi* how he once listened dutifully to a tedious defense of the much-maligned Arkansas mosquito by a long-winded Arkansan:

> These mosquitoes had been persistently represented as being formidable and lawless; whereas "the truth is, they are feeble, insignificant in size, diffident to a fault, sensitive"—and so on, and so on; you would have supposed he was talking about his family. But if he was soft on the Arkansas mosquitoes, he was hard enough on the mosquitoes of Lake Providence [Louisiana] to make up for it.... He said that two of them could whip a dog, and that four of them could hold a man down; and except help come, they would kill him. . . . He told many remarkable things about those lawless insects. Among others, said he had seen them try to *vote.* Noticing that this statement seemed to put a good deal of strain on us, he modified it a little; said he might have been mistaken as to that particular, but knew he had seen them around the polls "canvassing."

MOTHER

"I was always told that I was a sickly and precarious and tiresome and uncertain child," Mark Twain informed his biographer Paine, "and lived mainly on allopathic medicines during the first seven years of my life. I asked my mother about this, in her old age—she was in her eighty-seventh year—and said: 'I suppose that during all that time you were uneasy about me?' "

"Yes, the whole time," said she.

"Afraid I wouldn't live?"

After a reflective pause—ostensibly to think out the facts— "No—afraid you would."

MOTHER-IN-LAW

Mark Twain taught that there are two types of humor, conscious humor and unconscious humor. He used the following mother-in-law joke as an example of unconscious humor.

> A man receives a telegram telling him that his mother-in-law is dead and asking, "Shall we embalm, bury, or cremate her?"
> He wired back, "If these fail, try dissection."

"Now, the unconscious humor of this," Mark Twain explained, "was that he thought they'd try all of the three means suggested, anyway."

MOTIVE

There is *no* act, large or small, fine or mean, which springs from any motive but the one—the necessity of appeasing and contenting one's own spirit.

—"What Is Man?" essay, 1906

MURDERS

More books are written than are published, and far more books are dreamed of than are written. One book that Mark Twain dreamed of writing was a sensational murder mystery to be penned in collaboration with his friend William Dean Howells. It would be called *Twelve Memorable Murders,* and it would be published serially in a magazine, with a fresh murder every month to keep up reader interest. The two authors believed such a book would make them a fortune, but the scheme came to naught.

Twelve Memorable Murders was never written. Howells told Twain's biographer many years later, with a twinge of regret, "We never killed a single soul."

MUSIC

Music is a salve for the wounds of the soul, and everyone, no matter how devoid of musical talent, has sometime suffered from a yearning to play an instrument. Often, the lesser the talent, the greater the yearning. Mark Twain once succumbed to this temptation himself. "After a long immunity from the dreadful insanity that moves a man to become a musician in defiance of the will of God," he recalled, "I finally fell a victim to the instrument that they call the accordion."

He learned to play "Auld Lang Syne" on it. "After I had been playing 'Lang Syne' about a week, I had the vanity to think I could improve the original melody, and I set about adding some little flourishes and variations to it." He was soon driven out of his boardinghouse because of the vehement objections of the other boarders. He moved to another boardinghouse and was driven out of that one as well. After moving into his third boardinghouse in a week, the determined amateur musician once more resumed playing "Auld Lang Syne."

"The very first time I struck up the variations, a haggard, careworn, cadaverous old man walked into my room and stood beaming upon me a smile of ineffable happiness. Then he placed his hand upon my head, and looking devoutly aloft, he said with feeling unction, and in a voice trembling with emotion, 'God bless you, young man! God bless you! For you have done that for me which is beyond all praise. For years I have suffered from an incurable disease, and knowing my doom was sealed and that I must die, I have striven with all my power to resign myself to my fate, but in vain—the love of life was too strong within me. But heaven bless you, my benefactor! for since I heard you play that tune and those variations, I do not want to live any longer—I am entirely resigned—I am willing to die—in fact, I am anxious to die.' "

Wagner's music is better than it sounds.

—Paine, *Autobiography*, 1924, vol. 1, p. 337

It was new, and ought to have been rehearsed a little more. For some reason or other the queen had the composer hanged, after dinner.

—*A Connecticut Yankee*, 1889, ch. 17

I suppose there are two kinds of music—one kind which one feels, just as an oyster might, and another sort which requires a higher faculty, a faculty which must be assisted and developed by teaching. Yet if base music gives us wings, why should we want any other?

—*A Tramp Abroad,* 1880, vol. 1, ch. 24

MYSTERY

When we remember we are all mad, the mysteries of life disappear and life stands explained.

—Notebook, 1898

NAKED

A woman's reaction to the sight of an unidentified naked man is recorded in Mark Twain's notebook in 1888.

" 'And such a sight as he was,' said she. 'There he sat, almost stark naked—not a thing on but a pair of spectacles.' Paused and added, musingly, 'and one of *them* was broke, and you could see him right through it.' "

NAMES

In the Garden of Eden, it was Eve who named everything, according to Mark Twain's "Adam's Diary." Adam, who had not yet been formally introduced to Eve and merely referred to her as "the new creature," was utterly bewildered by her behavior.

"The new creature names everything that comes along, before I can get in a protest. And always the same pretext is offered—it *looks* like the thing. There is the dodo, for instance. Says the moment one looks at it one sees at a glance that it 'looks like a dodo. . . .' Dodo! It looks no more like a dodo than I do!"

Names are not always what they seem. The common Welsh name Bzjxxlwcp is pronounced Jackson.

—*Following the Equator,* 1897, vol. 1, ch. 36

We called him Barney for short. We couldn't use his real name. There wasn't time.

—*Following the Equator,* 1897, vol. 2, ch. 8

What remarkable names those diseases have! It makes me envious of the man that has them all.

—"Osteopathy," speech, 1901

NARRATIVE

"In writing, it is usually stronger and more dramatic to have a man speak for himself than to have someone else relate a thing about him," Mark Twain told a New York audience during a question-and-answer session after a lecture.

"Suppose a man dies," someone asked. "Is it stronger to have the man himself say that he has died?"

"Sometimes," Mark Twain answered. "Take the case of Major Patterson, down in Missouri, when a squatter had moved in on some of the extensive lands he had laid claim to. Deciding to use the frightening method to get the squatter off, the Major donned a mask one dark night, mounted an enormous black horse, rode to the squatter's door, called him out, and asked for a bucket of water. The Major had also availed himself of a contrivance . . . a large leather bag on his chest and stomach, buttoned securely under his coat.

"When the squatter had brought the water the Major raised the three-gallon bucket, slowly poured its contents into the bag through an opening at his throat, turned to the astonished squatter and said, 'Ah-h-h— That's the first drink of water I've had since I was killed at the battle of Shiloh!'

"The squatter disappeared from that part of the country,"
Mark Twain concluded. "And I think you will agree that when
the Major spoke for himself, the effect was stronger than otherwise."

NAST, THOMAS

No one knew better than Thomas Nast, the famous cartoonist,
how troublesome a houseguest was Mark Twain. On Thanksgiving Day, 1884, Twain dined at Nast's home in Morristown, New
Jersey, devouring five plates of oysters on the half shell. Staying
overnight in Nast's back room, Twain, who suffered from insom-
nia, was annoyed by the ticking of the hall clock, so he got up,
silenced it, and returned to bed. Then he was disturbed by the
ticking of the studio clock, so he got up and snuffed that out.
Everyone overslept in the morning because no alarm sounded, and
when Nast investigated he discovered that every clock in the
house had been stopped. When he confronted the culprit, Twain
shrugged.

"Well, those clocks were all overworked, anyway. They will
feel much better after a night's rest."

A few days later, Nast sent Twain a caricature drawing of the
humorist in his nightshirt battling with the diabolical clocks.

NATIONALISM

Each nation *knowing* it has the only true religion and the only sane
system of government, each despising all the others, each an ass
and not suspecting it.

—"What Is Man?" essay, 1906

NATURE

All things have their uses and their part and proper place in
Nature's economy: the ducks eat the flies—the flies eat the
worms—the Indians eat all three—the wild cats eat the Indians—
the white folks eat the wild cats—and thus all things lovely.

—*Roughing It,* 1872, ch. 38

Architects cannot teach nature anything.

—"Memorable Midnight Experience,"
essay, 1874

If you should rear a duck in the heart of the Sahara, no doubt it would swim if you brought it to the Nile.

—Attributed

NECESSITY

Necessity is the mother of "taking chances."

—*Roughing It,* 1872, ch. 42

Necessity knows no law.

—*Innocents Abroad,* 1869, ch. 51

NEIGHBORS

Mark Twain had been postponing a social call upon some new neighbors, but one day he saw an opportunity. "My name is Clemens," he said, bowing politely. "We ought to have called on you before, and I beg your pardon for intruding now in this informal way, but your house is on fire."

NEW DEAL

"F.D.R. told me that he took his famous phrase from M.T.'s *Connecticut Yankee* when I presented him our Mark Twain Gold Medal, 3rd December 1933," wrote Cyril Clemens, editor of *The Mark Twain Journal,* a leading scholarly organ.

The phrase that gave a name to Franklin Delano Roosevelt's administration was drawn from a chapter entitled "Freemen!" in which the Connecticut Yankee, who is basically an updated Jeffersonian democrat with technocratic tendencies, confronts the backward realities of the medieval monarchy and decides it is high time for a revolution. "And now here I was in a country where a right to say how the country should be governed was restricted to six persons in each thousand of its population," he observed. "I was to become a stockholder in a corporation where nine hundred and ninety-four of the members furnished all the money and did all the work, and the other six elected themselves a permanent board of direction and took all the dividends. It seemed to me that what the nine hundred and ninety-four dupes needed was a new deal."

A Connecticut Yankee in King Arthur's Court was less popular with the critics than *Tom Sawyer* and *Huckleberry Finn*, but Mark Twain considered it his magnum opus; it is the clearest and most complete statement of the author's democratic, egalitarian philosophy. The book was artistically flawed because the author inserted so much of his own opinion into it and did not disguise himself behind the mask of artistic irony as successfully as he did in *Huckleberry Finn*. In *Huckleberry Finn*, the author's views are so artfully masked that to this day there are some blacks who consider that book racist. But nobody will ever accuse the Connecticut Yankee, or his creator, of being a monarchist. *A Connecticut Yankee* is a literary manifesto for democratic revolution.

"It's my swan song, my retirement from literature," Mark Twain wrote sadly to his friend Howells. "Well, my book is written—let it go, but if it were only to write over again there wouldn't be so many things left out. They burn in me . . . but now they can't ever be said; and besides they would require a library— and a pen warmed up in hell."

NEW ENGLAND

"I am a Connecticut Yankee by adoption," said Mark Twain in an 1881 speech at a dinner of the New England Society. "In me, you have Missouri morals, Connecticut culture. This, gentlemen, is the combination which makes the perfect man."

NEW ENGLAND WEATHER

At a dinner of the New England Society in December 1876, the master of ceremonies offered a toast to "the oldest inhabitant— the weather of New England. Who can lose it and forget it? Who can have it and regret it? 'Be interposer 'twixt us twain.' "Responding to this quotation from *The Merchant of Venice*, Twain arose and delivered a paean to the "inhuman perversity" of the New England weather.

"I reverently believe that the Maker who made us all makes every thing in New England but the weather," he began.

"There is a sumptuous variety about the New England weather that compels the stranger's admiration—and regret. The weather is always doing something there; always attending strictly to business; always getting up new designs and trying them on people to see how they will go. But it gets through more business in spring than in any other season. In the spring I have counted one hundred and thirty-six different kinds of weather inside four-and-twenty hours."

The New England spring is something that cannot be understood by those who have not lived through it, Twain insisted. "The people of New England are by nature patient and forbearing but there are some things which they will not stand. Every year they kill a lot of poets for writing about 'Beautiful Spring.' These are generally casual visitors who bring their notions of spring from somewhere else."

Twain proceeded to point out the extreme difficulty that forecasters have in predicting the weather in New England. "One of the brightest gems in the New England weather is the dazzling uncertainty of it. There is only one certain thing about it. You are certain to have plenty of it."

But predicting the quality of the weather is much harder than predicting the quantity. "You fix up for the drought, you leave your umbrella in the house and sally out, and two to one you get drowned. You make up your mind that the earthquake is due, you stand from under and take hold of something to steady yourself, and the first thing you know you get struck by lightning."

Mark Twain found this New England weather forecast to be generally applicable: "Probable nor'east to sou'west winds, varying to the southward and westard and eastard and points between; high and low barometer, sweeping round from place to place; probable areas of rain, snow, hail, and drought, succeeded or preceded by earthquakes with thunder and lightning."

Then he added, "But it is possible that the programme may be wholly changed in the mean time."

Twain concluded his tribute to the New England weather with a personal note. "I could speak volumes about the inhuman perversity of the New England weather but I will give you but a single specimen. I like to hear rain on a tin roof. So I covered part of my roof with tin, with an eye to that luxury. Well, sir, do you think it ever rains on that tin? No, sir. Skips it every time."

NEWSPAPERS

Mark Twain lived in a time when people depended on newspapers for most of their information about what was going on in the world. He thought the public was too willing to believe the half-truths printed in newspapers. In an 1872 speech on "The Sins of the Press," he gave this example:

"A Detroit paper once said that I was in the constant habit of beating my wife and that I still kept this recreation up although I had crippled her for life and she was no longer able to keep out of my way when I came home in my usual frantic frame of mind. Now scarcely the half of that was true."

There are only two forces that can carry light to all the corners of the globe—only two—the sun in the heavens and the Associated Press down here.

—"Simplified Spelling," speech, 1906

The trouble is that the stupid people—who constitute the grand overwhelming majority of this and all other nations—do believe and are moulded and convinced by what they get out of a newspaper.

—"License of the Press," speech, 1873

I made a most thoughtful, symmetrical and admirable argument. But a Michigan newspaper editor answered, refuted it, utterly demolished it by saying I was in the constant habit of horsewhipping my great grandmother.

—Speech at a Republican rally, 1879

The old saw says, "Let a sleeping dog lie." Right. Still when there is much at stake it is better to get a newspaper to do it.

—*Following the Equator,* 1897, vol. 2, ch. 8

NEW YEAR'S RESOLUTIONS

At a New Year's party, Mark Twain was asked if he was making any resolutions for the coming year.

"Indeed," was his resolute reply. "I'm going to live within my income this year even if I have to borrow money to do it."

NEW YORK

When Mark Twain returned to New York after nine years abroad, a dinner was held in his honor at Delmonico's restaurant in December 1900. "In this absence of nine years I find a great improvement in the city of New York," said Twain to the assembled guests. "Some say it has improved because I have been away."

He paused a while and then added: "Others, and I agree with them, say it has improved because I have come back."

I, a virtuous person only a year before, after immersion for one year—during one year in the New York morals—had no more conscience than a millionaire.

—"New York Morals," speech, 1906

All men in New York insult you—there seem to be no exceptions. There are exceptions of course—*have* been—but they are probably dead.

—Notebook, 1885

NEW YORKERS

A New Yorker once chided Mark Twain: "You Missouri people are all right, but you're too provincial."

"Provincial?" retorted Twain. "On the contrary. Nobody in New York knows anything about Missouri, but everybody in Missouri knows all about New York."

There is a godless grace, and snap, and style about a born-and-bred New Yorker which mere clothing cannot effect.

—*Life on the Mississippi,* 1883, ch. 22

NIETZSCHE

Nietzsche published his book, and was at once pronounced crazy by the world—by a world which included tens of thousands of bright, sane men who believed exactly as Nietzsche believed but concealed the fact and scoffed at Nietzsche.

—Notebook, 1907

NOAH

The more I see of modern marine architecture and engineering the more I am dissatisfied with Noah's Ark. . . . Nobody but a farmer could have designed such a thing, for such a purpose.

—Notebook, 1896

NOBILITY

Mark Twain's lecture tour of England in 1873 was very successful, but one thing was lacking to make the triumph complete: the presence in the audience of some great member of the nobility. Near the end of his tour, Twain told a London audience he had "applied to a party at the East-end who is in the same line of business as Madame Tussaud, and he agreed to lend me a couple of Kings and some nobility, and he said that they would sit out my lecture, and not only sit it out, but that they wouldn't even leave the place when it was done, but would just stay where they were, perfectly infatuated, and wait for more."

Unfortunately, a mishap occurred when they were attempting to move Henry VIII into the lecture hall: "The porter fell downstairs and utterly smashed him all to pieces." A similar fate befell the other members of the royal party, dashing Twain's hopes of a noble turnout. He apologized humbly to his London audience for his lack of nobility, and added, "I wish I could get a king somewhere, just only for a little while, and I would take good care of him, and send him home, and pay the cab myself."

I will say this much for the nobility: that, tyrannical, murderous, rapacious and morally rotten as they were, they were deeply and enthusiastically religious.

—*A Connecticut Yankee*, 1889, ch. 16

NOVELISTS

There is only one expert who is qualified to examine the souls and the life of a people and make a valuable report— the native novelist.

—"What Paul Bourget Thinks of Us,"
essay, 1895

How much of his competency is derived from conscious "observation"? The amount is so slight that it counts for next to nothing in the equipment. Almost the whole capital of the novelist is the slow accumulation of *unconscious* observation—absorption.

—"What Paul Bourget Thinks of Us,"
essay, 1895

OBITUARY

On October 24, 1903, the British humorist Henry Lucy landed in New York, where he was handed a note from Mark Twain, which said: "You arrive this morning, and I sail this afternoon to avoid you." Twain was in fact departing that day for Florence.

Reporters asked Lucy to explain the note, and he obliged. "Some time ago Mark Twain and I were at a surprise dinner to E. A. Abbey, when he proposed to me that we start a newspaper called *The Obituary*. We were to print the life of every living man of prominence, send him the proof, and ask him for 50 pounds for suppressing the story. I considered the matter and wrote to Twain that it was agreeable to me. Since then he has made every effort, and successfully, to keep out of my way."

Indecency, vulgarity, obscenity—these are strictly confined to man; he invented them. Among the higher animals there is no trace of them.

—"The Lowest Animal," essay, 1897

OCCUPATIONS

Mark Twain tried out a number of different occupations before he discovered his true calling. "I had studied law an entire week, and then given it up because it was so prosy and tiresome. I had engaged briefly in the study of blacksmithing, but wasted so much time trying to fix the bellows so that it would blow itself, that the master turned me adrift in disgrace," he recalled in *Roughing It.* "I had been a bookseller's clerk for a while, but the customers bothered me so much I could not read with any comfort, and so the proprietor gave me a furlough and forgot to put a limit on it. I had clerked in a drug store part of a summer, but my prescriptions were unlucky, and we appeared to sell more stomach pumps than soda water. So I had to go.

"I had made of myself a tolerable printer, under the impression that I would be another Franklin some day, but somehow had missed the connection thus far." He had become a river pilot, only to have the river traffic cut off by the Civil War. Then he went west. "I had been a private secretary, a silver miner and a silver mine operative, and amounted to less than nothing in each, and now—what to do next?"

Unable to find honest work in Nevada, he tried journalism next, and the rest is literary history.

OLD AGE

When Mark Twain was a young man, he got into an argument about the purpose of life with an old man. The old fellow, failing to prevail in the debate, fell back upon the venerable authority of age.

"Young man, look at these gray hairs," he said.

"When a man gets to be as old as you I think he ought to dye," replied Twain. Noting the old man's displeasure at this answer,

Twain added: "You needn't think those gray hairs are any sign of wisdom; it's only a sign that your system lacks iron. I advise you to go home and swallow a crowbar."

We can't reach old age by another man's road. My habits protect my life but they would assassinate you.

—Seventieth-birthday speech, 1905

I am an old man and have known a great many troubles, but most of them never happened.

—Attributed

OPERA

Mark Twain was never quite comfortable with opera: "I dislike the opera because I want to love it and can't." He regarded it with the same suspicion with which he regarded the paintings of the great masters; he knew that appreciation was expected, even required, but he rebelled against the obligation. While he was living in Germany in 1891, he made a valiant effort to appreciate Wagner, whose music, he believed, was "better than it sounds." This is how he saw *Parsifal:*

"In 'Parsifal' there is a hermit named Gurnemanz who stands on the stage in one spot and practices by the hour, while first one and then another character of the cast endures what he can of it and then retires to die." Twain endured what he could of it and then he retired too.

"I have witnessed and greatly enjoyed the first act of everything which Wagner created, but the effect on me has always been so powerful that one act was quite sufficient; whenever I have witnessed two acts I have gone away physically exhausted; and whenever I have ventured an entire opera the result has been the next thing to suicide."

Twain concluded that the fault was in himself that he could not enjoy what was considered fine art. "Whenever I enjoy anything in art it means that it is mighty poor," he said sadly. "However, my base instinct does bring me profit sometimes; I was the only man out of 3,200 who got his money back on those operas."

OPINIONS

The following inscription appears beneath Mark Twain's bust in the Hall of Fame for Great Americans in New York City:

"Loyalty to petrified opinions never yet broke a chain or freed a human soul."

This quotation is drawn from a speech delivered in Hartford in 1884 and published as an essay entitled "Consistency" in 1923. The entire sentence in context reads: "Loyalty to petrified opinions never yet broke a chain or freed a human soul in this world— and never will."

Its name is Public Opinion. It is held in reverence. It settles everything. Some think it is the voice of God.

—"Corn-pone Opinions," essay, 1923

In all matters of opinion our adversaries are insane.

—*Christian Science,* 1907, bk. 1, ch. 5

Hardly a man in the world has an opinion upon morals, politics, or religion which he got otherwise than through his associations and sympathies. Broadly speaking, there are none but corn-pone opinions. And broadly speaking, corn-pone stands for self-approval. Self-approval is acquired mainly from the approval of other people. The result is conformity.

—"Corn-pone Opinions," essay, 1923

I am not one of those who in expressing opinions confine themselves to facts.

—"Wearing White Clothes," speech, 1907

It were not best that we should all think alike; it is difference of opinion that makes horseraces.

—*Pudd'nhead Wilson,* 1894, ch. 19

OPPORTUNITY

I was seldom able to see an opportunity until it had ceased to be one.

—Neider, *Autobiography,* 1959, ch. 44

ORIGINALITY

To give birth to an idea—to discover a great thought—an intellectual nugget, right under the dust of a field that many a brain plow had gone over before. To find a new planet, to invent a new hinge, to find the way to make the lightnings carry your messages. To be the *first*—that is the idea. To do something, say something, see something, before *anybody* else—these are the things that confer a pleasure compared with which all other pleasures are tame and commonplace, other ecstasies cheap and trivial.

—*Innocents Abroad,* 1869, ch. 26

PATENT ADJUSTABLE SPEECH

Mark Twain endured enough dull after-dinner speeches to bore a lesser man to death. Observing that many speeches consisted simply of two or three anecdotes "set in the midst of a lot of rambling and incoherent talk," he conceived the idea of an all-purpose speech that would be suitable for any occasion. He called it the "Patent Adjustable Speech." It had to be modified only slightly to fit different circumstances.

The Patent Adjustable Speech had two principal parts. There was a rousing statement to rally the crowd—"Agriculture, sir [or matrimony or religion or freedom of the press] is after all the palladium of our . . . liberties"—and one amusing anecdote with which to conclude, for example:

"And how felicitously what I have just been saying is illustrated in the case of the man who reached home at two o'clock in the morning and his wife said plaintively, 'Oh, John, when

you've had whiskey enough why don't you ask for sarsaparilla?'
And he said, 'Why, Maria, when I have had whiskey enough I
can't *say* sarsaparilla.' "

PATRIOTISM

"Majority Patriotism is the customary patriotism," said Mark
Twain. Americans too often teach their children to despise those
who hold unpopular opinions: "We teach them to regard as trai-
tors, and hold in aversion and contempt, such as do not shout with
the crowd, and so here in our democracy we are cheering a thing
which of all things is most foreign to it and out of place—the
delivery of our political conscience into somebody else's keeping.
This is patriotism on the Russian plan."

In the beginning of a change the patriot is a scarce man, and brave,
and hated and scorned. When his cause succeeds, the timid join
him, for then it costs nothing to be a patriot.

—Notebook, 1904

I would not voluntarily march under this country's flag, or any
other, when it was my private judgment that the country was in
the wrong.

—Paine, *Autobiography*, 1924, vol. 2, p. 18

My kind of loyalty was loyalty to one's country, not to . . . its
office-holders.

—*A Connecticut Yankee*, 1889, ch. 13

The modern patriotism, the true patriotism, the only rational patriotism is loyalty to the *nation* all the time, loyalty to the government when it deserves it.

—"The Czar's Soliloquy," essay, 1905

PEOPLE

There is a great deal of human nature in people.

—Walker, *Mark Twain's Travels with
Mr. Brown*, 1940, p. 185

If to be interesting is to be uncommonplace, it is becoming a question with me, if there *are* any commonplace people.

—"Refuge of the Derelicts," story, 1905

They talk to me about themselves, and about each other. Thus I get the entire man—four fifths of him from himself and the other fifth from the others. I find that no man discloses the completing fifth himself.

—"Refuge of the Derelicts," story, 1905

I know all those people. I have friendly, social, and criminal relations with the whole lot of them.

—"Taxes and Morals," speech, 1906

In my experience hard-hearted people are very rare everywhere.

—Paine, *Autobiography*, 1924, vol. 1, p. 125

The more you join in with people in their joys and their sorrows, the more nearer and dearer they come to be to you. . . . But it is sorrow and trouble that brings you the nearest.

—*Tom Sawyer Abroad*, 1894, ch. 11

PESSIMISM

Pessimist: The optimist who didn't arrive.

—Johnson, *More Maxims of Mark*, 1927, p. 12

The man who is a pessimist before 48 knows too much; if he is an optimist after it, he knows too little.

—Paine, *Mark Twain: A Biography*, 1912, vol. 2, p. 744 (maxim written on his 48th birthday)

PHYSICIANS

He has been a doctor a year now, and has had two patients—no, three, I think; yes, it *was* three. I attended their funerals.

—*The Gilded Age*, 1873, ch. 10

PLACES

The first time I ever saw St. Louis, I could have bought it for six million dollars, and it was the mistake of my life that I did not do it.

—*Life on the Mississippi*, 1883, ch. 22

Franklin was sober because he lived in Philadelphia. Why, Philadelphia is a sober city today. . . . Why, it is as good as Sunday to be in Philadelphia now.

—"Author and Publisher," speech, 1887

Newport, Rhode Island, that breeding place—that stud farm, so to speak—of aristocracy; aristocracy of the American type.

—Neider, *Autobiography*, 1959, ch. 57

Now I could give the reader a vivid description of the Big Trees and the marvels of the Yosemite—but what has this reader done to me that I should persecute him?

—*Roughing It*, 1872, ch. 61

A street in Constantinople is a picture which one ought to see once—not oftener.

—*Innocents Abroad*, 1869, ch. 33

Athens by moonlight! The prophet that thought the splendors of the New Jerusalem were revealed to him surely saw this instead! Overhead the stately columns, majestic still in their ruin . . . under foot the dreaming city . . . in the distance the silver sea.

—*Innocents Abroad*, 1869, ch. 32

PLAGIARISM

One Sunday morning, after attending church services in Hartford, Mark Twain approached Dr. Doane, the minister, and said jovially, "I enjoyed your service this morning, doctor. I welcomed it like an old friend. In fact, I have at home a book containing every word of it."

The minister was indignant. "You have not!"

"Yes, I have," insisted Twain.

"I would like to see it!" said Dr. Doane, huffily.

"I will send it to you," promised Mark Twain.

The following day, a messenger delivered to the Reverend Doane a copy of an unabridged dictionary.

PLEASURE

The exercise of an extraordinary gift is the supremest pleasure in life.

—*The American Claimant,* 1892, ch. 6

The lowest intellect, like the highest, possesses a skill of some kind and takes a keen pleasure in testing it, proving it, perfecting it.

—DeVoto, *Letters from the Earth,* 1962,
Letter 2

Riding aloft on a mountain of fragrant hay. This is the earliest form of the human pleasure excursion, and for utter joy and perfect contentment it stands alone in a man's threescore years and ten; all that come after it have flaws, but this has none.

—"Down the Rhone," essay, 1923

POETRY

When Mark Twain took over as editor of the *Buffalo Express* in 1869, he wrote an editorial in which he made a solemn pledge to the readers: "I shall not write any poetry unless I conceive a spite against the subscribers."

POLITICS

Mark Twain often criticized corrupt politicians, lamenting the low morals of public officials. "It's so hard to find men of a so high type of morals," he said, "that they'll *stay bought.*"

While living in New York, Twain made many pointed remarks about corruption at Tammany Hall. After the death of a certain Tammany leader, Twain told a newspaper reporter: "I refused to attend his funeral. But I wrote a very nice letter explaining that I approved of it."

To lodge all power in one party and keep it there is to insure bad government and the sure and gradual deterioration of the public morals.

—Paine, *Autobiography*, 1924, vol. 2, p. 14

An honest man in politics shines more than he would elsewhere.

—*A Tramp Abroad*, 1880, vol. 1, ch. 9

POLYGAMY

Mark Twain was once engaged by a Mormon in a debate on polygamy. The Mormon did most of the talking as he spared no argument in defense of the practice. Finally, he invoked the Bible: "I'll wager you can't cite a single passage in the Bible which forbids polygamy!"

"Sure I can," replied Mark Twain. " 'No man can serve two masters.' "

PONY EXPRESS

During the preceding night an ambushed savage had sent a bullet through the pony-rider's jacket, but he had ridden on, just the same, because pony-riders were not allowed to stop and inquire into such things unless killed.

—*Roughing It*, 1872, ch. 9

POPULARITY

Everybody's private motto: It's better to be popular than right.

—Notebook, 1902

POPULATION

What, then, Is the grand result of all this microbing and sanitation and surgery? . . . In time there will not be room in the world for the people to stand, let alone sit down.

Eve, in "Papers of the Adam Family,"
in DeVoto, *Letters from the Earth,* 1962

POSTAL SERVICE

People have been complaining about slow mail service ever since the dark ages. Mark Twain once noted that it had taken a letter from Ohio eleven days to reach him in New York. He remarked, "I owe a friend a dozen chickens, and I believe it will be cheaper to send eggs instead, and let them develop on the road."

POVERTY

When Mark Twain was a struggling young writer in San Francisco, living from hand to mouth, a lady of his acquaintance caught a glimpse of him standing outside the window of a restaurant, holding a cigar box under his arm.

"Mr. Clemens!" she confronted him. "Everywhere you go I see you with a cigar box under your arm. I'm afraid you smoke too much for your own good."

"It isn't that," said Twain. "You see, I'm moving again."

Honest poverty is a gem that even a King might feel proud to call his own, but I wish to sell out. . . . I wish to become rich, so that I can instruct the people and glorify honest poverty a little, like those kind-hearted, fat, benevolent people do.

—Walker, *Mark Twain's Travels with
Mr. Brown,* 1940, p. 236

In prosperity we are popular; popularity comes easy in that case, but when the other thing comes our friends are pretty likely to turn against us.

—*The American Claimant,* 1892, ch. 12

PRAYER

When you got to the table, you couldn't go right to eating, but you had to wait for the widow to tuck down her head and grumble a little over the victuals, though there warn't really anything the matter with them.

—Huckleberry Finn, 1884, ch. 1

Then Miss Watson she took me in the closet and prayed, but nothing came of it. She told me to pray every day, and whatever I asked for I would get it. But it warn't so. I tried it. Once I got a fish-line, but no hooks. It warn't any good to me without hooks.

—Huckleberry Finn, 1884, ch. 3

If you would beseech a blessing upon yourself, beware! lest without intent you invoke a curse upon a neighbor at the same time.

—"War Prayer," dictated 1904,
published 1923

The average clergyman, in all countries and of all denominations, is a very bad reader. One would think he would at least learn how to read the Lord's Prayer, by and by, but it is not so. He races through it as if he thought the quicker he got it in, the sooner it would be answered.

—A Tramp Abroad, 1880, ch. 36

PREACHER

Mark Twain seriously considered becoming a preacher. He was saved by a job offer from the *Territorial Enterprise* in Nevada, which arrived just when he "stood upon the verge of the ministry or the penitentiary." Later, when he lost his newspaper job in San Francisco, he described himself as "once more penniless and pointed for the ministry." The ministry appealed to him because "it never occurred to me that a preacher could be damned. It looked like a safe job." But he ultimately decided against it because he "lacked one thing—the stock in trade, i.e. religion."

Nevertheless, Twain frequently referred to his lecturing as "preaching." Early in his career, the California press, perhaps dimly recognizing a new American prophet, began referring to him humorously as "St. Mark."

I have always preached. . . . If the humor came of its own accord and uninvited I have allowed it a place in my sermon, but I was not writing the sermon for the sake of the humor. I should have written the sermon just the same, whether any humor applied for admission or not.

—Neider, *Autobiography*, 1959, ch. 55

He was a preacher, too . . . and never charged nothing for his preaching, and it was worth it, too.

—*Huckleberry Finn*, 1884, ch. 33

PREJUDICE

Their opinions were all just green with prejudice.

—Seventieth-birthday speech, 1905

Where prejudice exists it always discolors our thoughts.

—Neider, *Autobiography*, 1959, ch. 77

PRESIDENTIAL CAMPAIGN

During Mark Twain's mock presidential campaign of 1880, he poked fun at politicians.

"My financial views are of the most decided character," he said, mimicking the false candor of the conventional candidate, "but they are not likely, perhaps, to increase my popularity with the advocates of inflation."

Further elaborating on his economic policies, he said, "I do not insist upon the special supremacy of rag money or hard money. The great fundamental principle of my life is to take any kind I can get."

With regard to his poverty program, Mark Twain was much more forthright than most other presidential candidates. "I regard the poor man, in his present condition, as so much wasted raw material. Cut up and properly canned, he might be made useful to fatten the natives of the cannibal islands and to improve our export trade in that region," said Twain. "My campaign cry will be: 'Desiccate the poor workingman; stuff him into sausages.' "

Other politicians tried to conceal the skeletons in their closets, but not this candid candidate. "I admit that I treed a rheumatic grandfather of mine in the winter of 1850," he confessed. And he added: "The rumor that I buried a dead aunt under my grapevine was correct. The vine needed fertilizing."

I don't mind what the opposition say of me so long as they don't tell the truth about me.

—Speech at a Republican rally, 1880

PRESS

Its mission . . . is to stand guard over a nation's liberties, not its humbugs and shams.

—*The American Claimant,* 1892, ch. 10

PRICE

During the tour of the Holy Land described in *Innocents Abroad,* Mark Twain frequently exasperated the deacons with his blasphemous remarks.

But when the party was informed of the exorbitant price for a boat on the Sea of Galilee, even those pilgrims who had traveled halfway around the world to sail on the sacred water balked at paying the bill.

"Well," said Twain to his fellow travelers, "Do you wonder now that Christ walked?"

PRINCIPLES

Principles have no real force except when one is well fed.

—Adam, in "Adam's Diary," 1893

Principles aren't of much account, anyway, except at election time.

—"The Anti-Doughnut Party," speech, 1901

PRISON

"Being in jail has its advantages," Mark Twain told an audience of prisoners in Pretoria, South Africa, in 1896. "A lot of great men have been in jail. If Bunyan had not been in jail, he would never have written 'Pilgrim's Progress.' Then the jail is responsible for 'Don Quixote.' " Twain informed the prisoners they were better off in jail, that they would probably have ended up there anyhow, that being in jail was easier than working for a living, and that he would use his influence to double their sentences.

Some of the prisoners failed to perceive the irony of his remarks, and a riot nearly ensued. Twain had to explain that he was joking, which was quite uncharacteristic of him, and then the inmates calmed down.

PROFANITY

In certain trying circumstances, urgent circumstances, desperate circumstances, profanity furnishes a relief denied even to prayer.

—Paine, *Mark Twain: A Biography*,
1912, vol. 1, p. 214

What a lie it is to call this a free country, where none but the unworthy and undeserving may swear.

—"Speech-Making Reform," speech,
1885

PROHIBITION

Taking the pledge will not make bad liquor good, but it will improve it.

—Johnson, *More Maxims of Mark*, 1927,
p. 13

The more things are forbidden, the more popular they become.

—Notebook, 1895

When men want drink, they'll have it in spite of all the laws ever passed.

—Notebook, 1895

Temperate temperance is best. Intemperate temperance injures the cause of temperance, while temperate temperance helps it in its fight against intemperate intemperance. Fanatics will never learn that, though it be written in letters of gold across the sky.

—*Notebook*, 1896

PROMISES

I never could keep a promise. I do not blame myself for this weakness, because the fault must lie in my physical organization. It is likely that such a very liberal amount of space was given to the organ which enables me to *make* promises that the organ which should enable me to keep them was crowded out.

—*Innocents Abroad*, 1869, ch. 23

Great enterprises usually promise vastly more than they perform.

—*Innocents Abroad*, 1869, conclusion

To make a pledge of any kind is to declare war against nature; for a pledge is a chain that is always clanking and reminding the wearer of it that he is not a free man.

—*Following the Equator*, 1897, vol. 1, ch. 1

To promise not to do a thing is the surest way in the world to make a body want to go and do that very thing.

—*Tom Sawyer*, 1876, ch. 22

PROPHECY

Prophecy: Two bull's eyes out of a possible million.

—Johnson, *More Maxims of Mark*, 1927, p. 12

He could foretell wars and famines, though that was not so hard, for there was always a war and generally a famine somewhere.

—"The Mysterious Stranger," story, 1916, ch. 1

A genuine expert can always foretell a thing that is five hundred years away easier than he can a thing that's only five hundred seconds off.

—A Connecticut Yankee, 1889, ch. 27

PROPHET

Mark Twain often told stories about how other people told stories. One example was the story of a small boy's story of the prophet Elijah.

"There was once a prophet named Elijah," said the lad. "One day he was going up a mountain. Some boys threw stones at him. He said, 'If you keep throwing stones at me I'll set the bears on you and they'll eat you up.' And they did, and he did, and the bears did."

One of the entries in *Pudd'nhead Wilson's Calendar* refers to that story:

"There is this trouble about special providences—namely, there is so often a doubt as to which party was intended to be the beneficiary. In the case of the children, the bears, and the prophet, the bears got more real satisfaction out of the episode than the prophet did, because they got the children."

PROSPERITY

Prosperity is the best protector of principle.

—Following the Equator, 1897, vol. 2, ch. 2

It does rather look as if in a republic where all are free and equal, prosperity and position constitute rank.

—The American Claimant, 1892, ch. 12

Few of us can stand prosperity—another man's, I mean.

—Following the Equator, 1897, vol. 2, ch. 4

PSYCHOLOGY

In the matter of psychologizing, a professional is too apt to yield to the fascinations of the loftier regions of that great art, to the neglect of its lowlier walks.

—"What Paul Bourget Thinks of Us,"
essay, 1895

PUBLIC INTEREST

Do I seem to be seeking the good of the world? That is the idea. It is my public attitude; privately I am seeking my own profit. We all do it but it is sound and it is virtuous, for no public interest is anything other or nobler than a massed accumulation of private interests.

—"Simplified Spelling," speech, 1906

PUBLISHERS

Mark Twain told in his autobiography of his difficulty in selling his first book. On one occasion, he was admitted to a publisher's office only because of a misunderstanding, which was soon cleared up. "When he found that I had come to sell a book and not to buy one, his temperature fell sixty degrees and the old-gold intrenchments in the roof of my mouth contracted three-quarters of an inch and my teeth fell out."

Twenty-one years after this publisher threw Mark Twain out of his office, he met the world-famous author and apologized: "I refused a book of yours and for this I stand without competitor as the prize ass of the nineteenth century."

"It was a most handsome apology and I told him so," recalled Twain, who then confided to him: "During the lapsed twenty-one years I had in fancy taken his life several times every year and always in new and increasingly cruel and inhuman ways . . . but thenceforth I should hold him my true and valued friend and never kill him again."

Authors sometimes understand their side of the question but this is rare; none of them understands the publisher's side of it.

—Neider, *Autobiography*, 1959, ch. 57

All publishers are Columbuses. The successful author is their
America. The reflection that they—like Columbus—didn't discover what they expected to discover, didn't discover what they
started out to discover, doesn't trouble them.

—Neider, *Autobiography*, 1959, ch. 50

PUNCTUATION

Along with a manuscript he was submitting to a publisher, Mark
Twain attached a note:

"Gentlemen:.,;?!()"---*'.. Please scatter these throughout according to your taste."

PUNISHMENT

"When I was a youngster I attended school at a place where the
use of the birch rod was a hallowed tradition," recollected Mark
Twain. "It was against the rules to mark the desks in any manner,
the penalty being a fine of $3 or public chastisement.

"Happening to violate the rule on one occasion, I was offered
the choice. I told my father about it, and as he seemed to think
it would be too bad for me to be publicly punished, he gave me
the $3. Now at that period of my existence $3 was a large sum,
while a whipping was of little consequence, and so—" Here
Twain paused thoughtfully and flicked a few ashes from his cigar.
"And so, that was how I earned my first $3."

All crimes should be punished with humiliations—public expo-
sure in ridiculous and grotesque situations—and never in any
other way. Death makes a hero of the villain, and he is envied by
some spectators and by imitators.

—Notebook, 1888

PUNS

Many puns have been made on Mark Twain's name, but the only
one Mark Twain himself would admit to was delivered in London

at the Authors Club in 1899. The pun came at the end of a tribute to Rudyard Kipling, whose illness in New York had aroused the sympathy of Britons and Americans alike.

Twain said he was exhausted because he had spent the last eight days "compiling a pun" and this was it: "Since England and America have been joined in Kipling, may they not be severed in Twain."

RACE

Samuel Clemens, although not a college graduate himself, paid for the college education of two gifted black men, one of whom graduated from Yale Law School and became a judge; the other graduated from a Southern seminary and became a minister. Clemens did not do this as a publicity stunt; in fact, he made no mention of it anywhere in his writings. It was not until 1985 that a Yale scholar unearthed documentary proof of Clemens's tuition payments and a letter to the dean of Yale explaining his motives. It was a partial payment of the reparation "due from every white man to every black man" for having perpetrated the crime of slavery.

There are many humorous things in the world; among them the white man's notion that he is less savage than the other savages.

—*Following the Equator*, 1897, vol. 1, ch. 21

Nearly all black and brown skins are beautiful, but a beautiful white skin is rare.

—*Following the Equator,* 1897, vol. 2, ch. 5

One of my theories is that the hearts of men are about alike, no matter what their skin-complexions may be.

—Letter to Alvert Sonnichsen, 1901

RADICAL

The radical of one century is the conservative of the next. The radical invents the views. When he has worn them out the conservative adopts them.

—Notebook, 1898

RAILROAD

Mark Twain often complained about the slow railroad service in foreign countries. In Egypt, he estimated that the trains must have been built around the time of the pyramids. "I shall not speak of the railway, for it is like any other railway—I shall only say that the fuel they use for the locomotive is composed of mummies three thousand years old, purchased by the ton or by the graveyard for that purpose, and that sometimes one hears the profane engineer call out pettishly, 'Damn these plebeians, they don't burn worth a cent—pass out a King!' "

It was one of those trains that gets tired every seven minutes and stops to rest three quarters of an hour. . . . Next year we will walk.

—Letter to Mrs. Crane, September 18, 1892

A railroad is like a lie—you have to keep building to it to make it stand.

—Walker, *Mark Twain's Travels with Mr. Brown,* 1940, p. 146

RAIN

As Mark Twain and his friend William Dean Howells were leaving church one Sunday morning, a heavy rain commenced.

"Do you think it will stop?" Howells asked.

Mark Twain answered, "It always has."

REASONING

Man is the Reasoning Animal. Such is the claim. I think it is open to dispute.

—"The Lowest Animal," essay, 1897

Two things which are the peculiar domain of the heart, not the mind—politics and religion. He doesn't want to know the other side. He wants arguments and statistics for his own side, and nothing more.

—Notebook, 1896

Often, in matters concerning religion and politics, a man's reasoning powers are not above the monkey's.

—"Last Visit to England," in DeVoto,
Mark Twain in Eruption, 1940

REFLECTION

Reflection is the beginning of reform. There can be no reform without reflection. If you don't reflect when you commit a crime then that crime is of no use. It might just as well have been committed by someone else.

—"The Watermelon," speech, 1907

REFORM

Mark Twain, at the urging of his wife, was continually trying to reform and lead a better life. An entry from his journal in 1896, when he was on a ship in the Indian Ocean, shows what a strain it was for him:

"Swore off from profanity early this morning—I was on deck in the peaceful dawn, the calm of holy dawn. Went down, dressed, bathed, put on white linen, shaved—a long, hot, trouble-some job and no profanity. Then started to breakfast. Remem-bered my tonic—first time in three months without being told—poured it into a measuring-glass, held bottle in one hand, it in the other, the cork in my teeth . . . ship lurched, heard a crash behind me—it was the tumbler, broken into millions of fragments, but the bottom hunk whole. Picked it up to throw out of the open port, threw out the measuring glass instead—then I released my voice. Mrs. Clemens behind me in the door.

" 'Don't reform any more. It is not an improvement.' "

Nothing so needs reforming as other people's habits.

—*Pudd'nhead Wilson,* 1894, ch. 15

That desire which is in us all to better other people's condition by having them think as we think.

—"What Is Man?" essay, 1906

Every time I reform in one direction, I go overboard in another.

—Quoted in *Sacramento Union,* 1866

REGRETS

Mark Twain once declined an invitation with these regrets: "In bed with a chest cold and other company."

REINCARNATION

Mark Twain believed in reincarnation. Once, he surprised his audience by mentioning an incident that occurred the first time he was in Egypt and casually dropping the remark: "This was four or five thousand years ago." Pausing and noting the perplexity of his audience, he continued: "I am speaking of a former state of existence of mine, perhaps my earliest reincarnation; indeed I think it was the earliest. I had been an angel previously, and I am expecting to be one again."

I have been born more times than anybody except Krishna.

—Neider, *Autobiography,* 1959, ch. 46

RELIGION

When Mark Twain was living in Riverdale, New York, he was befriended by Mr. Carstensen, a liberal-minded local minister. One evening, Mr. Carstensen invited Twain to accompany him to town to dine with a party that included a Catholic bishop, an Indian Buddhist, and a Chinese scholar of the Confucian creed, after which they were all going to a Yiddish theater.

Twain was impressed by the multiethnic composition of this party. He said, "Well, there's only one thing you need to make the party complete—that is, either Satan or me."

Man—he is the only animal that loves his neighbor as himself, and cuts his throat if his theology isn't straight.

—"The Lowest Animal," essay, 1897

So much blood has been shed by the Church because of an omission from the Gospel: "Ye shall be *indifferent* as to what your neighbor's religion is." . . . Divinity is claimed for many religions; but no religion is great enough or divine enough to add that new law to its code.

—Paine, *Mark Twain: A Biography*,
1912, vol. 3, p. 1537

Man . . . is kind enough when he is not excited by religion.

—"A Horse's Tale," story, 1906

Grown people everywhere are always likely to cling to the religion they were brought up in.

—*Following the Equator*, 1897, vol. 2, ch. 15

If you know a man's nationality you can come within a split hair of guessing the complexion of his religion.

—"What Is Man?" essay, 1906

They was all Moslems, Tom said, and when I asked him what a Moslem was, he said it was a person that wasn't a Presbyterian.

So there is plenty of them in Missouri, though I didn't know it before.

—Huck Finn, in *Tom Sawyer Abroad*, 1894, ch. 13

Religion consists in a set of things which the average man thinks he believes, and wishes he was certain.

—Notebook, 1879

Creeds mathematically precise and hair-splitting niceties of doctrine are absolutely necessary for the salvation of some kinds of souls.

—*Innocents Abroad*, 1869, ch. 25

Many of these people have the reasoning faculty, but no one uses it in religious matters.

—Satan, in DeVoto, *Letters from the Earth*, 1962, Letter 3

It took several thousand years to convince our fine race—including every splendid intellect in it—that there is no such thing as a witch; it has taken several thousand years to convince that same fine race—including every splendid intellect in it—that there is no such person as Satan.

—"Is Shakespeare Dead?" essay, 1909

If man continues in the direction of enlightenment, his religious practice may, in the end, attain some semblance of human decency.

—"Bible Teaching and Religious Practice," essay, 1923

The altar-cloth of one aeon is the doormat of the next.

—Notebook, 1898

Now I only pray that there may be a God—and a heaven—or something better.

—"Which Was the Dream?" story, 1897

"Answer the gentleman, Thomas—don't be afraid."

Tom still hung fire.

"Now I know you'll tell *me*," said the lady. "The names of the first two disciples were—"

"DAVID AND GOLIATH!"

Let us draw the curtain of charity over this scene.

—*Tom Sawyer*, 1876, ch. 4
(Tom Sawyer in Sunday school)

REPARTEE

Repartee is something we think of twenty-four hours too late.

—Attributed

REPENTANCE

Repentance ain't confined to doing wrong, sometimes you catch it just as sharp for doing right.

—"Refuge of the Derelicts," story, 1905

Often when we repent of a sin, we do it perfunctorily, from principle, coldly and from the head; but when we repent of a good deed the repentance comes hot and bitter and straight from the heart.

—"Something About Repentance," in
DeVoto, *Letters from the Earth*, 1962

REPETITION

I thoroughly believe that any man who's got anything worthwhile to say will be heard if he only says it often enough.

—"A Humorist's Confession," *New York Times*, 1905

REPUBLICAN

No one has ever seen a Republican mass meeting that was devoid of the perception of the ludicrous.

—"Turncoats," speech, 1885

People seem to think they are citizens of the Republican party and that that is patriotism and sufficiently good patriotism. I prefer to be a citizen of the United States.

—Notebook, 1888

REPUTATION

Reputation is a hall-mark: it can remove doubt from pure silver, and it can also make the plated article pass for pure.

—Unmailed letter written around 1886

RESPECT

When people do not respect us we are sharply offended; yet in his private heart no man much respects himself.

—*Following the Equator,* 1897, vol. 1, ch. 29

RESPECTABILITY

And he grew up and married, and raised a large family, and brained them all with an ax one night, and got wealthy by all manner of cheating and rascality; and now he is the infernalest wickedest scoundrel in his native village, and is universally respected, and belongs to the legislature.

—"The Bad Little Boy," story, 1865

REVERENCE

Reverence for one's own sacred things—parents, religion, flag, laws, and respect for one's own beliefs—these are feelings which we cannot even help. They come natural to us; they are involuntary, like breathing. There is no personal merit in breathing.

—*Following the Equator,* 1897, vol. 2, ch. 17

But the reverence which is difficult, and which has personal merit in it, is the respect which you pay, without compulsion, to the political or religious attitude of a man whose beliefs are not yours.

—*Following the Equator,* 1897, vol. 2, ch. 17

REVOLUTION

Wherefore there is no longer a nobility, no longer a privileged class, no longer an Established Church: all men are become exactly equal, they are upon one common level, and religion is free. *A republic is hereby proclaimed,* as being the natural estate of a nation.

—*A Connecticut Yankee,* 1889, ch. 42
(Hank Morgan announcing his revolution)

I am a revolutionist by birth, reading and principle. I am always on the side of the revolutionists because there never was a revolution unless there were some oppressive and intolerable conditions against which to revolute.

—*New York Sun, Tribune, World,* 1906
(in defense of Maxim Gorki)

When we consider that not even the most reasonable English monarchs ever yielded back a stolen public right until it was wrenched from them by bloody violence, is it rational to suppose that gentler methods can win privileges in Russia?

—"Letter to the Editor of Free
Russia," 1890

The first gospel of all monarchies should be Rebellion; the second should be Rebellion; and the third and all gospels, and the only gospel of any monarchy, should be Rebellion—against Church and State.

—Notebook, 1891

RICHES

Like all the other nations, we worship money and the possessors of it—they being our aristocracy. . . . We like to read about rich people in the papers; the papers know it, and they do their best to keep this appetite liberally fed. . . . "Rich Woman Fell Down Cellar—Not Hurt." The falling down the cellar is of no interest to us when the woman is not rich, but no rich woman can fall down cellar and we not yearn to know all about it and wish it was us.

—*Autobiography* excerpt, *North American Review,* 1907

If all men were rich, all men would be poor.

—Notebook, 1898

Pleasure, Love, Fame, Riches: they are but temporary disguises for lasting realities—Pain, Grief, Shame, Poverty.

—"The Five Boons of Life," story, 1902

Those riches which are denied to no nation on the planet—humor and feeling.

—Letter to William White, June 24, 1906

RICHMOND

Mark Twain was visiting Richmond, Virginia, one day when he complained of an acute pain in his stomach.

"It can't be the air or the food you ate in Richmond," said a proud native of the Old Dominion. "There's no healthier city in America than Richmond. Our death rate is only one person per day."

"Run over to the newspaper office," requested Twain, "and find out if today's victim has died yet."

RIDICULE

No god and no religion can survive ridicule. No church, no nobility, no royalty or other fraud, can face ridicule in a fair field and live.

—Notebook, 1888

RIGHT

Always do right. This will gratify some people, and astonish the rest.

—Note to Young People's Society, 1901

Do right and you will be conspicuous.

—Paine, *Mark Twain: A Biography,*
1912, vol. 3, p. 1134

Do right *for your own sake,* and be happy in knowing that your *neighbor* will certainly share in the benefits resulting.

—"What Is Man?" essay, 1906

RIGHT AND WRONG

In *Huckleberry Finn,* the young hero is confused over the issue of right and wrong. He has been taught that slavery is right and stealing is wrong, and his conscience tells him what he has always been taught. Mark Twain believed that conscience was often only the voice of conformity.

"Thinks I, this is what comes of my not thinking. Here was this nigger, which I had as good as helped to run away, coming right out flat-footed and saying he would steal his children— children that belonged to a man I didn't even know; a man that hadn't ever done me no harm."

But Huck's heart tells him that slavery is wrong and he is right to help Jim escape from it. One path hurts his conscience, the other hurts his heart. He decides to follow the path of his heart.

"What's the use you learning to do right when it's troublesome to do right and ain't no trouble to do wrong, and the wages is just the same?"

Huckleberry Finn overrules his conscience and helps Jim escape, even though he believes he is doing the wrong thing. He ascribes his sinfulness to poor early training.

"I see it warn't no use for me to try to learn to do right; a body that don't get *started* right when he's little ain't got no show."

RIVER PILOT

Mark Twain was a Mississippi River pilot from 1857 to 1860, when the Civil War put an end to the riverboat traffic. He took his pen name from the river pilots' slang term for two fathoms, a safe depth. "I love the profession far better than any I have

followed since, and I took a measureless pride in it," he wrote in
Life on the Mississippi. "The reason is plain: a pilot, in those days,
was the only unfettered and entirely independent human being
that lived in the earth."

Your true pilot cares nothing about anything on earth but the
river, and his pride in his occupation surpasses the pride of kings.

—*Life on the Mississippi,* 1883, ch. 7

In truth, every man and woman and child has a master, and
worries and frets in servitude; but in the day I write of, the
Mississippi pilot had *none.*

—*Life on the Mississippi,* 1883, ch. 14

By the Shadow of Death, but he's a lightning pilot!

—*Life on the Mississippi,* 1883, ch. 7
(a river compliment)

And if he can do such gold-leaf, kid-glove, diamond-breastpin
piloting when he is sound asleep, what *couldn't* he do if he was
dead!

—*Life on the Mississippi,* 1883, ch. 11
(of a sleep-walking pilot)

RIVERS

Mark Twain was proud of his Mississippi past, and he took an
almost proprietary pride in the river and its magnitude, "a mon-
strous big river," "its mile-wide tide rolling along, shining in the
sun." In *Life on the Mississippi,* he declares, "It is the longest river
in the world," and proceeds to describe its dimensions in spell-
binding detail. So proud was Twain of the Mississippi that he
could not keep from belittling any other river whose reputation
overflowed its banks.

He scoffed at the Arno, the pride of Italy: "It is popular to
admire the Arno. It is a great historical creek with four feet in the
channel and some scows floating around. It would be a very
plausible river if they could pump some water into it."

Of the Guires River, a tributary of the Rhone in Europe, he wrote disparagingly: "Later I took a twilight tramp along the high banks of a moist ditch called the Guires River. If it was my river I wouldn't leave it outdoors nights, in this careless way, where any dog can come along and lap it up."

He thumbed his nose at the Neckar, the principal river of Germany: "A hatful of rain makes high water in the Neckar, and a basketful produces an overflow."

Nor did he restrict his mockery to foreign rivers. He could not take any other American river seriously beside the Mississippi. He put down the Platte River of Nebraska: "The Platte was 'up,' they said—which made me wish I could see it when it was down, if it could look any sicker and sorrier."

And of the Humboldt River in Nevada, Twain said disdainfully, "One of the pleasantest and most invigorating exercises one can contrive is to run and jump across the Humboldt River until he is overheated, and then drink it dry."

For Mark Twain, no river could possibly compare favorably with the Mississippi.

ROMANCE

To be human is to have one's little modicum of romance secreted away in one's composition. One never ceases to make a hero of one's self—in private.

—*The Gilded Age*, 1873, ch. 10

The romance of life is the only part of it that is overwhelmingly valuable, and romance dies with youth.

—*Mark Twain's Letters to Will Bowen*, 1941, p. 27

ROYALTY

The institution of Royalty in any form is an insult to the human race.

—Notebook, 1888

Let us take the present male sovereigns of the earth—and strip them naked. Mix them with 500 naked mechanics, and then march the whole around a circus ring, charging suitable admission of course—and desire the audience to pick out the sovereigns. They couldn't. You would have to paint them blue. You can't tell a king from a cooper except you differentiate their exteriority.

—Notebook, 1888

SALARY

As a young man in the West, Mark Twain worked at a variety of occupations. In *Roughing It,* he tells how his career in quartz milling came to an end when he asked for a salary increase:

"I only remained in the milling business one week. I told my employer I could not stay longer without an advance in my wages; that I liked quartz milling, indeed was infatuated with it; that I had never before grown so tenderly attached to an occupation in so short a time; that nothing, it seemed to me, gave such scope to intellectual activity as feeding a battery and screening tailings, and nothing so stimulated the moral attributes as retorting bullion and washing blankets—still, I felt constrained to ask for an increase of salary."

He did not get the raise.

SALT LAKE CITY

Salt Lake City was healthy—an extremely healthy city. They declared there was only one physician in the place and he was arrested every week regularly and held to answer under the vagrant act for having "no visible means of support."

—*Roughing It,* 1872, ch. 13

SAN FRANCISCO

In his old age, when his traveling days were done, Mark Twain declined an invitation to return to San Francisco for a reunion. He sent this tactful letter of regrets:

"I have done more for San Francisco than any other of its old residents. Since I left there, it has increased in population fully 300,000. I could have done more—I could have gone earlier—it was suggested."

SATAN

Satan is a recurring character in Mark Twain's works. Sometimes he is called Satan by name, as in "The Mysterious Stranger" and "Letters from the Earth." In other stories, such as "The Man That Corrupted Hadleyburg" or "The War Prayer," the Satanic character is simply an unidentified "stranger," often one who speaks with a darkly prophetic voice. Mark Twain made Satan a spokesman for the "other side," giving voice to the doubts and despair of the human being in conflict, telling the unpleasant truths that people do not want to hear.

"I have always felt friendly toward Satan," wrote Mark Twain in his autobiography. "Of course that is ancestral; it must be in the blood, for I could not have originated it."

Mark Twain discusses Satan at length in an 1899 essay about prejudice, "Concerning the Jews." He sees Satan as the eternal victim of prejudice, superstition and slander.

"I have no special regard for Satan; but I can at least claim that I have no prejudice against him. It may even be that I lean a little his way, on account of his not having a fair show," declares Mark Twain. "All religions issue bibles against him, and say the most injurious things about him, but we never hear *his* side."

Perhaps Satan is not guilty, after all. Perhaps Satan is merely the scapegoat of our own evil. "Of course Satan has some kind of a case, it goes without saying. It may be a poor one, but that is nothing; that can be said about any of us."

Satan never got a fair trial, Mark Twain reminds us. "We have none but the evidence for the prosecution, and yet we have rendered the verdict. To my mind, this is irregular. It is un-English. It is un-American; it is French."

Twain vowed to look into Satan's case, along with Shakespeare's, in the afterlife. "As soon as I can get at the facts I will undertake his rehabilitation myself," he promised, "if I can find an unpolitic publisher."

In the meantime, Satan deserves a little more respect. "We may not pay him reverence, for that would be indiscreet, but we can at least respect his talents. A person who has for untold centuries maintained the imposing position of spiritual head of four-fifths of the human race, and political head of the whole of it, must be granted the possession of executive abilities of the loftiest order."

Satan hasn't a single salaried helper; the Opposition employs a million.

—Notebook, 1898

But who prays for Satan? Who, in eighteen centuries, has had the common humanity to pray for the one sinner that needed it most?

—Neider, *Autobiography*, 1959, ch. 7

SCIENCE

There ain't no way to find out why a snorer can't hear himself snore.

—*Tom Sawyer Abroad*, 1894, ch. 10

Scientists have odious manners, except when you prop up their theory; then you can borrow money of them.

—"As Concerns Interpreting the Deity," essay, 1917

The scientist. He will spend thirty years in building up a mountain range of facts with the intent to prove a certain theory; then he is so happy in his achievement that as a rule he overlooks the main chief fact of all—that his accumulation proves an entirely different thing.

—"The Bee," essay, 1917

A scientist will never show any kindness for a theory which he did not start himself.

—*A Tramp Abroad*, 1880, vol. 2, ch. 14

We know all about the habits of the ant, we know all about the habits of the bee, but we know nothing at all about the habits of the oyster. It seems almost certain that we have been choosing the wrong time for studying the oyster.

—*Pudd'nhead Wilson*, 1894, ch. 16

SEASICKNESS

During an Atlantic crossing in foul weather, Mark Twain fell victim to seasickness. Afterward, describing the experience to a friend, he said there are two distinct stages of seasickness: "At first you are so sick you are afraid you will die, and then you are so sick you are afraid you won't die."

We all like to see people sea-sick when we are not ourselves.

—*Innocents Abroad*, 1869, ch. 3

SELF-APPROVAL, GOSPEL OF

Mark Twain wrote a booklet called "What Is Man?" which he had privately printed in 1906 and distributed among his friends. He called it his "Gospel of Self-Approval." The central idea is that man is always "looking out for No. 1" and cannot do otherwise, for that is human nature. "Man's sole impulse," according to Twain, is "the securing of his own self-approval." Therefore we should try to elevate our ideals and standards for self-approval, striving toward self-improvement, rather than trying to become

unselfish—which is impossible—and hypocritically pretending to be "looking out for No. 2," which is standard procedure.

We ignore and never mention the Sole Impulse which dictates and compels a man's every act: the imperious necessity of securing his own approval. . . . To it we owe all that we are.

—"What Is Man?" essay, 1906

SERMON

One of the secrets of successful public speaking is knowing when to stop. Mark Twain illustrates this point with the following recollection:

"Many years ago in Hartford, we all went to church one hot, sweltering night to hear the annual report of Mr. Hawley, a city missionary who went around finding people who needed help and didn't want to ask for it. He told of the life in cellars, where poverty resided; he gave instances of the heroism and devotion of the poor. 'When a man with millions gives,' he said, 'we make a great deal of noise. It's a noise in the wrong place, for it's the widow's mite that counts.' Well, Hawley worked me up to a great pitch. I could hardly wait for him to get through. I had $400 in my pocket. I wanted to give that and borrow more to give. You could see the greenbacks in every eye. But instead of passing the plate then, he kept on talking and talking and talking, and as he talked it grew hotter and hotter and hotter, and we grew sleepier and sleepier and sleepier. My enthusiasm went down, down, down—$100 at a clip—until finally, when the plate did come around, I stole ten cents out of it."

Few sinners are saved after the first twenty minutes of a sermon.

—*Hannibal Courier-Post,* March 6, 1835

SEX

"It is not immoral to create the human species—with or without ceremony," Mark Twain told Albert Bigelow Paine. "Nature intended exactly these things."

Mark Twain believed that the advance of civilization made inevitable the ultimate equality of the sexes, but that women had so far been getting the short end of the stick sexually. Satan, the sarcastic spokesman of "Letters from the Earth," cited the example of Solomon to prove this point:

"Solomon, who was one of the Deity's favorites, had a copulation cabinet composed of seven hundred wives and three hundred concubines. To save his life he could not have kept two of these young creatures satisfactorily refreshed, even if he had fifteen experts to help him. Necessarily almost the entire thousand had to go hungry for years and years on a stretch. Conceive of a man hardhearted enough to look daily upon all that suffering and not be moved to mitigate it."

Now if you or any other really intelligent person were arranging the fairnesses and justices between man and woman, you give the man a one-fiftieth interest in one woman, and the woman a harem.

—Satan, in DeVoto, *Letters from the Earth*, 1962, Letter 8

The law of God, as quite plainly expressed in woman's construction, is this: There shall be no limit put upon your intercourse with the other sex sexually, at any time of life.

—Satan, in DeVoto, *Letters from the Earth*, 1962, Letter 8

Of the delights of this world man cares *most* for sexual intercourse. He will go any length for it—risk fortune, character, reputation, life itself. And what do you think he has done? He has left it out of his heaven! Prayer takes its place.

—Notebook, 1906

When Adam ate the apple in the Garden and learned how to multiply and replenish, the other animals learned the Art, too, by watching Adam. It was cunning of them, it was neat; for they got all that was worth having out of the apple without tasting it and afflicting themselves with the disastrous Moral Sense, the parent of all the immoralities.

—DeVoto, *Letters from the Earth*, 1962, Letter 4

Adam and Eve now knew what evil was, and how to do it. They knew how to do various kinds of wrong things, and among them one principal one—the one God had his mind on principally. That one was the art and mystery of sexual intercourse.

—After the Fall, in DeVoto, *Letters from the Earth*, 1962, Letter 3

SHAKESPEARE

Mark Twain, to his dying day, insisted that William Shakespeare did not write the great works ascribed to him; that the historical William Shakespeare was not a writer at all but a businessman—that "William Shakespeare" was, like "Mark Twain," only a pen name. Mark Twain's last book, published in 1909, was a long essay about the mystery of Shakespeare's identity, called "Is Shakespeare Dead?" For some unexplained reason, Twain told his literary executors that this essay was to be part of his autobiography, although no editor has yet taken this request literally.

In the essay, Mark Twain argues that there is no evidence to support a claim for Shakespearean authorship, and that what evidence there is about the historical personage named William Shakespeare does not suggest that he was a literary person. For example, Shakespeare's will left no mention of any books or manuscripts; and his epitaph is pure and unadulterated doggerel. "Shakespeare didn't know that he was a writer," Mark Twain said sarcastically, "and nobody told him until after he was dead."

Twain never committed himself as to the real identity of the author—he simply insisted that it was not William Shakespeare. Once, during a visit to London, he was invited to dinner by a group of Baconians who subscribed to the theory that the plays were written by Francis Bacon. When one of his hosts asked him who he thought the real author was, Mark Twain answered: "I'll wait until I get to Heaven and ask Shakespeare who did write his plays."

"I don't think, Mr. Clemens, that you will find Shakespeare in Heaven," said the Baconian, somewhat snootily.

Mark Twain replied, "Then *you* ask him."

So far as anybody actually knows and can prove, Shakespeare of Stratford-on-Avon never wrote a play in his life. So far as anybody knows and can prove, he never wrote a letter to anybody in his life. . . . So far as anybody knows and can prove, Shakespeare of Stratford-on-Avon wrote only one poem during his life. . . . He commanded that this work of art be engraved upon his tomb, and he was obeyed. There it abides to this day. This is it:

> Good friend for Jesus sake forbeare
> To digg the dust encloased heare;
> Blest be ye man yt spares thes stones
> And curst be he yt moves my bones.

—"Is Shakespeare Dead?" essay, 1909

SHOES

Mark Twain hated to see anybody walking out of the lecture hall when he was talking. Once, in Hamilton, Ohio, a man in squeaky shoes started to tiptoe toward the door. Twain called out to him: "Take off your shoes, please! Take off your shoes!"

SIN

To lead a life of undiscovered sin! That is true joy.

—"My Real Self," speech, 1900

It is the first wrong steps that count—How easy it is to go from bad to worse, when once we have started upon a downward course.

—"The $30,000 Bequest," story, 1904

There are many scapegoats for our sins, but the most popular is Providence.

—Notebook, 1898

All you have to do in order to become entirely pure is to commit all the sins there are. I have done that. Anybody can do it. Anybody can build up a perfect moral character.

—"Caprices of Memory," speech, 1908

The real life that I live and the real life that I suppose all of you live is a life of interior sin.

—"My Real Self," speech, 1900

A sin takes on new and real terrors when there seems a chance that it is going to be found out.

—"The Man That Corrupted
Hadleyburg," story, 1899

SINGING

One evening at a dinner party, some of the guests gathered around the piano and started singing songs. The hostess, noticing that Mark Twain was abstaining from this musical merriment, asked him if he did not sing.

He answered politely, "Those who have heard me say I don't."

SLANDER

A feeble, stupid, preposterous lie will not live two years—except it be a slander upon somebody.

—"Advice to Youth," speech, 1882

It is not wise to keep the fires going under a slander unless you can get some large advantage out of keeping it alive. Few slanders can stand the wear of silence.

—Neider, *Autobiography*, 1959, ch. 10

SLAVERY

In my schooldays I had no aversion to slavery. I was not aware that there was anything wrong about it. No one arraigned it in my hearing; the local papers said nothing against it; the local pulpit taught us that God approved it, that it was a holy thing.

—Neider, *Autobiography*, 1959, ch. 2

Lincoln's proclamation . . . not only set the black slaves free, but set the white man free also.

—Fourth of July speech, 1907

SLEEP

I am losing enough sleep to supply a worn-out army.

—Paine, *Mark Twain: A Biography,*
1912, vol. 3, p. 1569

Well enough for old folks to rise early, because they have done so many mean things all their lives they can't sleep anyhow.

—Notebook, 1866

SLOWNESS

Mark Twain was a notoriously slow man. He was famous for his slow, drawling speech, and those who met him were struck by his slow, unhurried movements and mannerisms. There was something casual, almost indolent about his way of walking, talking and conducting his business.

Sometimes his movements were so slow as to be almost imperceptible. This is illustrated by an incident that occurred during a tour of Madame Tussaud's Wax Museum on his visit to London in 1907.

Mark Twain was standing in silent meditation before a wax figure in the Chamber of Horrors, when he was suddenly poked in the ribs by a ruddy-cheeked Englishwoman with an umbrella. When he jumped, she screamed, "Oh Lor', it's alive!" and fled in terror.

I have seen slower people than I am—and more deliberate . . . and even quieter, and more listless, and lazier people than I am. But they were dead.

—"Memoranda," *Galaxy Magazine,*
December 1870

SMALL TOWNS

Human nature cannot be studied in cities except at a disadvantage—a village is the place. There you can know your man inside and out—in a city you but know his crust; and his crust is usually a lie.

—Notebook, 1883

SMOKING

When he was thirty-four and but lately married, Mark Twain, under the influence of his bride, ceased smoking for a year and a half. But in 1871, during the writing of *Roughing It,* he found it necessary to reinstate his regimen of smoking ten cheap cigars a day. He insisted that he was not a slave to the habit, however. "To cease smoking is the easiest thing," he declared. "I ought to know. I've done it a thousand times."

Moderation, however, was harder to achieve. On one occasion, he pledged to smoke only one cigar a day. "I kept the cigar waiting until bedtime, then I had a luxurious time with it. But desire persecuted me every day and all day long; so, within the week I found myself hunting for larger cigars . . . then larger ones still, and still larger ones. Within the fortnight I was getting cigars *made* for me—on still a larger pattern. They still grew and grew in size. Within the month my cigar had grown to such proportions that I could have used it as a crutch. It now seemed to me that a one-cigar limit was no real protection to a person, so I knocked my pledge on the head and resumed my liberty."

I have made it a rule never to smoke more than one cigar at a time.

—Seventieth-birthday speech, 1905

As an example to others, and not that I care for moderation myself, it has always been my rule never to smoke when asleep and never to refrain when awake.

—Seventieth-birthday speech, 1905

I have stopped smoking now and then . . . but it was not on principle, it was only to show off. It was to pulverize those critics who said I was a slave to my habits and couldn't break my bonds.

—Seventieth-birthday speech, 1905

SNORING

Mark Twain was a sound sleeper, and sometimes the sound of his sleeping kept other people awake. Other members of his household had tried every remedy to cure him of his snoring but banishment.

Once, on a week-long boat trip with friends, he inquired whether his nocturnal pneumatics kept anyone awake. "At breakfast," he said, "I ventured for the first time to throw out a feeler, for all these days' silence made me a little uneasy and suspicious. I intimated that at home, I sometimes snored—not often, and not much, but a little—yet it might be possible that at sea, I—though I hoped—that is to say—

"But I was most pleasantly interrupted at that point by a universal outburst of compliment and praise, with assurances that I made the nights enjoyable for everybody, and that they often lay awake hours to listen, and Mr. Rogers said it infused him so with comfortableness that he tried to keep himself awake by turning over and over in bed, so as to get more of it. Rice said it was not a coarse and ignorant snore. Colonel Payne said he was always sorry when the night was over and he knew he had to wait all day before he could have some more; and Tom Reed said the reason he moved down into the coal bunkers was because it was even sweeter there, where he could get a perspective on it. This is very different from the way I am treated at home, where there is no appreciation of what a person does."

SOCIETY

Mark Twain was once a guest of honor at an opera box party put on by a prominent member of New York society. The hostess felt at home at the opera and proceeded to talk throughout the performance—to Mark Twain's increasing annoyance.

After the opera was over, she turned to Twain and gushed, "Oh, my dear Mr. Clemens, I do hope you will be with us next Saturday. I just know you will enjoy it—the opera will be 'Tosca.' "

"How tantalizing," replied Mark Twain. "I've never heard you in that."

There are no common people except in the highest spheres of society.

—Fisher, *Abroad with Mark Twain,* 1922, p. 218

In England when one is with titled people the conversation is nearly exclusively about people with titles.

—Neider, *Autobiography*, 1959, ch. 76

SOUL

A great soul, with a great purpose, can make a weak body strong and keep it so.

—*Joan of Arc*, 1896, bk. 2, ch. 4

SOUP

Mark Twain loathed being served bean soup. He had a very particular palate and preferred to prepare certain dishes himself. After some bold experiments during a long sea voyage, he hit upon what he thought was the perfect recipe for bean soup:

"Take a lot of water, wash it well, and broil it until it is brown on both sides; then very carefully pour one bean into it and let it simmer. When the bean begins to get restless, sweeten it with salt, then put it up in air-tight cans, hitch each can to a brick, and chuck them overboard, and the soup is done."

SOUTH

Sir Walter [Scott] had so large a hand in making Southern character, as it existed before the [Civil] War, that he is in great measure responsible for the war.

—*Life on the Mississippi*, 1883, ch. 46

The educated Southerner has no use for an *r*, except at the beginning of a word.

—*Life on the Mississippi*, 1883, ch. 44

SPEECHMAKING

Mark Twain used to say he loved to hear himself talk, because he got so much moral instruction out of it, but that the joy was lost to him when he did it for hire. Nevertheless, he was one of the most successful professional speakers of his time—and of all time—and there were many years when he earned more from speaking than from writing.

No writer in history has ever been in such demand as a speaker. In fact, there is probably no other author in the history of literature who equaled Mark Twain's success as an orator. As Kurt Vonnegut has observed, "Twain was so good with crowds that he became, in competition with singers and dancers and actors and acrobats, one of the most popular performers of his time. It is so unusual, and so psychologically unlikely for a great writer to be a great performer, too, that I can think of only two similar cases—Homer's, perhaps, and Molière's."

Anyone interested in public speaking can pick up some useful pointers from Mark Twain. His basic technique was what he called the *counterfeit impromptu*—a carefully written and well-rehearsed speech that was delivered in such an offhand way as to appear impromptu. "It usually takes me three weeks to prepare an impromptu speech," he confessed.

But Mark Twain was best known as the master of "the pause." Many of his greatest punch lines were preceded by long, artful pauses. "I used to play with the pause as other children play with a toy," he said. The pause requires perfect timing, however. "If the pause is too short the impressive point is passed, and the audience have had time to divine that a surprise is intended—and then you can't surprise them."

Twain was opposed to the practice of reading literary works to an audience from the platform. "Written things are not for speech; their form is literary," he contended. "They have to be limbered up, broken up, colloquialized and turned into the common forms of unpremeditated talk—otherwise they will bore the house, not entertain it."

Instead of reading from a book, the speaker should *talk* to the audience. "In reading from the book you are telling another person's tale at second-hand; you are a mimic and not the person involved," noted Mark Twain in his *Autobiography*. "Whereas in telling the tale without the book you absorb the character and presently become the man himself, just as is the case with the actor."

For Mark Twain, public speaking was in fact a form of acting. "The greatest actor would not be able to carry his audience by storm with a book in his hand; reading from the book renders the nicest shadings of delivery impossible." The speaker's task was to create the illusion of talking spontaneously to the audience.

Mark Twain never shouted at his audiences, in the polemical manner of politicians and preachers. Firstly, he did not have the voice for it; his voice was naturally soft and low. More important, shouting shattered the illusion of spontaneous talk. It was an obvious oratorical device used by those who could not keep a crowd's attention in any other way. To Mark Twain, loudest was not best. As he wrote in *Pudd'nhead Wilson's New Calendar,* "Noise proves nothing. Often a hen who has merely laid an egg cackles as if she laid an asteroid."

Eloquence is the essential thing in a speech, not information.

—"3,000 Years Among the Microbes,"
story, 1905

The best and most telling speech is not the actual impromptu one but the counterfeit of it.

—"Plethora of Speeches," speech,
1884

That impromptu speech is most worth listening to which has been carefully prepared in private and tried on a plaster case or an empty chair or any other appreciative object that will keep quiet until the speaker has got his matter and his delivery limbered up so that they will seem impromptu to an audience.

—"Plethora of Speeches," speech,
1884

A person who is to make a speech at any time or anywhere, upon any topic whatever, owes it to himself and to his audience to write the speech out and memorize it.

—Neider, *Autobiography,* 1959, ch. 77

This is the way to get the attention of a fussy and excited young crowd. Start to say something; then pause; they notice *that,* though they hadn't noticed your words—nor cared for them, either. Their clack ceases; they set their eyes upon you, intently, expectantly.

—"3,000 Years Among the Microbes," story, 1905

The pause is an exceedingly important feature in any kind of story, and a frequently recurring feature, too. It is a dainty thing, and delicate, and also uncertain and treacherous; for it must be exactly the right length—no more and no less—or it fails of its purpose and makes trouble.

—"How to Tell a Story," essay, 1895

The right word may be effective, but no word was ever as effective as a rightly timed pause.

—Paine, *Mark Twain's Speeches,* 1923, p. xv

I have been cautioned to talk but be careful not to say anything. I do not consider this a difficult task.

—"Nineteenth Century Progress,"
speech, 1878

SPIRIT

Any so-called material thing that you want is merely a symbol: you want it not for *itself,* but because it will content your spirit for the moment.

—"What Is Man?" essay, 1906

Spirit . . . has fifty times the strength and staying-power of brawn and muscle.

—"Saint Joan of Arc," essay, 1904

STATESMANSHIP

If we had less statesmanship, we would get along with fewer battleships.

—Notebook, 1905

The true statesman does not despise any wisdom, howsoever lowly may be its origin.

—*A Connecticut Yankee,* 1889, ch. 26

STATISTICS

I've come loaded with statistics, for I've noticed that a man can't prove anything without statistics.

—Speech at a Republican rally, 1880

Sometimes half a dozen figures will reveal, as with a lightning-flash, the importance of a subject which ten thousand labored words, with the same purpose in view, had left at last but dim and uncertain.

—*Life on the Mississippi*, 1883, ch. 28

Figures often beguile me, particularly when I have the arranging of them myself; in which case the remark attributed to Disraeli would often apply with justice and force: "There are three kinds of lies: lies, damned lies, and statistics."

—Neider, *Autobiography*, 1959, ch. 28

STORYTELLING

Mark Twain's stories were so widely repeated that he sometimes found himself in the curious position of hearing one of his own tales told back to him. This happened to him in Australia in 1896. A clever gentleman sat down to talk with him at a club. "I saw in a moment that he was a person with a local story-telling reputation," Twain recorded in his notebook. "He began to remark on the slowness of the New Zealand railroad service and I saw that he was working up the atmosphere for an anecdote and presently he launched into the anecdote."

The storyteller told how he had advised the conductor to take the cowcatcher off the front of the train and put it at the other end of the train, "because we are not going to catch any cows, but there is no protection against their climbing aboard at the rear end of the train and biting the passengers."

Mark Twain could have embarrassed the storyteller by pointing out that there are no cowcatchers on Australian trains, but he didn't. "I could have embarrassed him still more, perhaps, by showing him that I had printed that little tale when he was a boy. In fact I invented it for use in a lecture a hoary, long time ago."

I like a good story well told. That is the reason I am sometimes forced to tell them myself.

—"The Watermelon," speech, 1907

If you wish to lower yourself in a person's favor, one good way is to tell his story over again, the way *you* heard it.

—Notebook, 1898

Most people who have the narrative gift—that great and rare endowment—have with it the defect of telling their choice things over the same way every time, and this injures them and causes them to sound stale and wearisome after several repetitions.

—*Joan of Arc,* 1896, ch. 7

There are few stories that have anything superlatively good in them except the *idea*—and that is always bettered by transplanting.

—Letter to William Dean Howells, 1876

STOVES

Mark Twain did not trust European stoves, which he regarded as inflammatory devices. He observed dryly: "In America we prefer to kindle the fire with the kerosene can and chance the inquest."

STRANGERS

During his days as a lecturer, Samuel Clemens arrived in a small midwestern town one afternoon and stepped into a barbershop to be shaved.

"You are a stranger in town, sir?" asked the barber.

"I am a stranger to *you*," answered Clemens.

"We're having a good lecture here tonight, sir," said the barber. "Mark Twain is coming to town. Are you going to see him?"

"Yes, I think I will," said Clemens.

"Have you got your ticket yet?" asked the barber.

"No, I'm afraid not," Clemens replied.

"Then I'm afraid you'll have to stand. The seats are all sold out."

"How annoying!" said Samuel Clemens. "I have the worst luck! It seems as if I always have to stand whenever I hear that man Twain lecture."

SUCCESS

The man with a new idea is a Crank until the idea succeeds.

—*Following the Equator,* 1897, vol. 1, ch. 32

Behold, the fool saith, "Put not all thine eggs in the one basket"— which is but a manner of saying, "Scatter your money and your attention;" but the wise man saith, "Put all your eggs in the one basket and—WATCH THAT BASKET."

—*Pudd'nhead Wilson,* 1894, ch. 15

It is strange the way the ignorant and inexperienced so often and undeservedly succeed when the informed and the experienced fail.

—Neider, *Autobiography,* 1959, ch. 45

All you need in this life is ignorance and confidence, and then Success is sure.

—Notebook, 1887

SUNDAY

Sunday. Pulled through. This day is getting to be more and more trying.
Monday. I believe I see what the week is for; it is to give time to rest up from the weariness of Sunday.

—Adam, in "Adam's Diary," story, 1893

SUNSET

One must stand on his head to get the best effect in a fine sunset, and set a landscape in a bold, strong framework that is very close at hand, to bring out all its beauty.

—Attributed

SUPERSTITION

Let me make the superstitions of a nation and I care not who makes its laws or its songs either.

—*Following the Equator,* 1897, vol. 2, ch. 15

When the human race has once acquired a superstition nothing short of death is ever likely to remove it.

—Neider, *Autobiography,* 1959, ch. 78

When even the brightest mind in our world has been trained up from childhood in a superstition of any kind, it will never be possible for that mind, in its maturity, to examine sincerely, dispassionately, and conscientiously any evidence or any circumstance which shall seem to cast a doubt upon the validity of that superstition. I doubt if I could do it myself.

—"Is Shakespeare Dead?" essay, 1909

SURGERY

Mark Twain offered this advice on the proper state of mind for undergoing surgery: "Console yourself with the reflection that you are giving the doctor pleasure, and that he is getting paid for it."

SWEARING

Mark Twain's habit of swearing was repulsive to his wife, who tried religiously to cure him of it. One day, while he was shaving, he cut himself and recited his entire liturgy of curses. When he finished, Livy, who was in the next room, shocked him by repeating what he had said, word for word.

"I wanted you to hear just how it sounded," she said sternly. Mark Twain winced. "It would pain me to think that when I swear it sounds like that," he said with chagrin. "You got the words right, but you don't know the tune."

The idea that no gentleman ever swears is all wrong. He can swear and still be a gentleman if he does it in a nice and benevolent and affectionate way.

—"Private and Public Morals,"
speech, 1906

The spirit of wrath—not the words—is the sin; and the spirit of wrath is cursing. We begin to swear before we can talk.

—*Following the Equator,* 1897, vol. 1, ch. 31

If I cannot swear in heaven I shall not stay there.

—Notebook, 1898

SWITZERLAND

Mark Twain was deeply impressed, even moved, by the quaint Swiss practice of yodeling, when he first encountered it. He described this pleasant experience in *A Tramp Abroad.* "Now the jodler appeared—a shepherd boy of sixteen— and in our gladness and gratitude we gave him a franc to jodl some more. So he jodled and we listened. We moved on, presently, and he generously jodled us out of sight. After about fifteen minutes we came across another shepherd boy who was jodling, and gave him half a franc to keep it up. He also jodled us out of sight. After that, we found a jodler every ten minutes; we gave the first one eight cents, the second one six cents, the third one four, the fourth one a penny, contributed nothing to Nos. 5, 6, and 7, and during the remainder of the day hired the rest of the jodlers, at a franc apiece, not to jodl any more. There is somewhat too much of this jodling in the Alps."

TALK

I cannot keep from talking, even at the risk of being instructive.

—"London," speech, 1872

The average man likes to hear himself talk when he is not under criticism.

—"A Ragged Ramshackle Vow,"
speech, 1882

Learning began with talk and is therefore older than books. Our opinions do not really blossom into fruition until we have expressed them to someone else.

—Read, *Mark Twain and I*, 1940, p. 38

Everybody talks about the weather, but nobody does anything about it.

—Attributed to Mark Twain and to Dudley Warner

TAXES

Tax time is the time that tries all men's souls. "I used to be an honest man," Mark Twain lamented in a 1906 speech at Carnegie Hall. "I have crumbled. When they assessed me at $75,000 a fortnight ago I went out and tried to borrow the money and couldn't. Then when I found they were letting a whole crop of millionaires live in New York at a third of the price they were charging me I was hurt, I was indignant, and said, 'This is the last feather. I am not going to run this town all by myself.' "

His moral disintegration complete, Mark Twain soon found himself standing before the tax officers. "And I lifted up my hand along with those seasoned and experienced deacons and swore off every rag of personal property I've got in the world, clear down to the cork leg, glass eye and what is left of my wig."

What is the difference between a taxidermist and a tax collector? Answer: A taxidermist takes only your skin.

—Notebook, 1902

We've got so much taxation. I don't know of a single foreign product that enters this country untaxed except the answer to prayer.

—"New York Morals," speech, 1906

TEACHING

I like to instruct people. It's noble to teach oneself. It is still nobler to teach others, and less trouble.

—"Doctor Van Dyke," speech, 1906

When a teacher calls a boy by his entire name it means trouble.

—Neider, *Autobiography*, 1959, ch. 8

TELEPHONE

Mark Twain recorded the following Christmas message on an early gramophone. The recording still exists, providing one of the few extant samples of Mark Twain's drawling speech:

"It is my heart-warm and world-embracing Christmas hope and aspiration that all of us, the high, the low, the rich, the poor, the admired, the despised, the loved, the hated, the civilized, the savage (every man and brother of us all throughout the whole earth), may eventually be gathered together in a heaven of everlasting rest and peace and bliss, except the inventor of the telephone."

Confound a telephone, anyway. It is the very demon for conveying similarities of sound that are miracles of divergence from similarity of sense.

—A Connecticut Yankee, 1889, ch. 23

TEMPER

It takes me a long time to lose my temper, but once lost I could not find it with a dog.

—Notebook, 1894

TEMPTATION

There are several good protections against temptations, but the surest is cowardice.

—Following the Equator, 1897, vol. 1, ch. 36

Lead us into temptation.

—"The Man That Corrupted
Hadleyburg," 1899
(revised motto of the corrupted town of Hadleyburg)

THANKSGIVING

Thanksgiving Day. Let all give humble, hearty, and sincere thanks, now, but the turkeys. In the island of Fiji they do not use turkeys; they use plumbers. It does not become you and me to sneer at Fiji.

—Pudd'nhead Wilson, 1894, ch. 18

THEORY

There's another trouble about theories: there's always a hole in them somewheres, sure, if you look close enough.

—Tom Sawyer Abroad, 1894, ch. 9

THINKING

It were not best that we should all think alike.

—Pudd'nhead Wilson, 1894, ch. 19

Men think they think upon the great political questions, and they do; but they think with their party, not independently; they read its literature, but not that of the other side.

—"Corn-pone Opinions," essay, 1923

It is because they do not think at all; they only think they think.

—Satan on mankind, in DeVoto,
Letters from the Earth, 1962, Letter 2

THOUGHT

Go by *thought.* If you went only as fast as light or electricity you would be forever getting to any place, heaven is so big.

—"Captain Stormfield's Visit to
Heaven," story, 1907

A man's private thought can never be a lie; what he thinks, is to him the truth, always.

—Letter to Louis Pendleton, August
4, 1888

Life does not consist mainly—or even largely—of facts and happenings. It consists mainly of the storm of thoughts that is forever blowing through one's head.

—Paine, Autobiography, 1924, vol. 1, p. 283

TIME

As a young man in the West, Mark Twain was often in debt. He once wrote to a creditor, quoting Benjamin Franklin's proverb:

"Time is money. Now, I haven't got any money, but, as regards time, I am in affluent circumstances, and if you will receipt that bill, I will give you a check for as much time as you think equivalent, and throw you in a couple of hours for your trouble."

There is in life only one moment and in eternity only one.

—Notebook, 1896

A round man cannot be expected to fit in a square hole right away. He must have time to modify his shape.

—"More Tramps Abroad," 1897

TOAST

In *Roughing It,* Mark Twain recalled how, at a dinner held in honor of the humorist Artemus Ward, the guest of honor lifted his glass solemnly and said, "I give you Upper Canada."

The company rose and drank the toast in reverent silence. Then Twain asked, "But why did you give us Upper Canada?"

"Because I don't want it myself," replied Artemus Ward gravely.

TRAINING

"Training is everything. The peach was once a bitter almond; cauliflower is nothing but cabbage with a college education." This entry in Pudd'nhead Wilson's calendar epitomizes Mark Twain's philosophy. A human being is a product of two factors: heredity and training. Since heredity cannot be altered after the fact, training is the only important variable in human success. Thus, training is everything: "Training is everything," says the Connecticut Yankee, "training is all there *is* to a person. We speak of nature; it is folly; there is no such thing as nature; what we call by that misleading name is merely heredity and training."

Training is not necessarily intentional; we are automatically trained by the environment in which we live and by our associations, which imprint themselves upon us. "All training is one form or another of *outside influence,* and *association* is the largest part of it," Twain asserted. The essential thing is to get good training instead of bad training: "Inestimably valuable is training, influence, education, in right directions."

No one can achieve anything important simply as a result of heredity or talent, according to Mark Twain. Training is always the critical factor in success: "Talent is useless without training, thank God."

When people assume responsibility for their own training, they are no longer programmed by their environment; they become the programmers. This strategy offers many benefits. "It gives you a splendid reputation with everybody to know that you get up with the lark," Mark Twain advised a group of young people in 1882. "And if you get the right kind of a lark and work at him right you can easily train him to get up at half past nine every time."

There is nothing that training cannot do. Nothing is above its reach or below it. It can turn bad morals to good, good morals to bad; it can destroy principles, it can recreate them; it can debase angels to men and lift men to angelship. And it can do any of these miracles in a year—even in six months.

—"As Regards Patriotism," essay,
1923

TRAINS

Mark Twain was not a patient traveler. Once, he found himself stuck on a slow train that stopped and hesitated every few hundred yards. He grew so incensed at the incessant delays that when the conductor came around, Mark Twain handed him a half fare, which was customarily used for children.

The conductor glared at him. "And are you a child?" he asked sarcastically.

"No, not any more," replied Mark Twain. "But I was when I got on your damn train!"

TRAVEL

Mark Twain was a seasoned traveler who learned to be skeptical of the many, many wonders of the world, many of which were not wonderful at all. For example, Twain said, "In a museum in Havana there are two skulls of Christopher Columbus, 'one when he was a boy and one when he was a man.' "

The gentle reader will never, never know what a consummate ass he can become until he goes abroad.

—Innocents Abroad, 1869, ch. 23

I have found out that there ain't no surer way to find out whether you like people or hate them than to travel with them.

—Tom Sawyer Abroad, 1894, ch. 11

I find that, as a rule, when a thing is a wonder to us it is not because of what *we* see in it, but because of what *others* have seen in it. We get almost all our wonders at second hand. . . . By and by you sober down, and then you perceive that you have been drunk on the smell of somebody else's cork.

—Following the Equator, 1897, vol. 2, ch. 17

St. Peter's, Vesuvius, Heaven, Hell, everything that is much described is bound to be a disappointment at first experience.

—Notebook, 1876

Travel and experience mar the grandest pictures and rob us of the most cherished traditions of our boyhood.

—Innocents Abroad, 1869, ch. 55

One can gorge sights to repletion as well as sweetmeats.

—Innocents Abroad, 1869, ch. 54

On the whole I think that short visits to Europe are better than long ones. The former preserve us from becoming Europeanized.

—A Tramp Abroad, 1880, vol. 2, ch. 21

Travel is fatal to prejudice, bigotry, and narrow-mindedness, and many of our people need it sorely on these accounts. Broad, wholesome, charitable views of men and things cannot be acquired by vegetating in one little corner of the earth all one's lifetime.

—*Innocents Abroad*, 1869, conclusion

It liberalizes the Vandal to travel. You never saw a bigoted, opinionated, stubborn, narrow minded, self-conceited, almighty mean man in your life but he had stuck in one place ever since he was born and thought God made the world and dyspepsia and bile for his especial comfort.

—"American Vandal Abroad," speech, 1868

TRUTH

"An old saying of mine has been misquoted," Mark Twain said at a New York banquet in 1906. "I didn't say: 'When in doubt, tell the truth.' What I did say was: 'When you are in doubt, tell the truth.' When I am in doubt, I use more sagacity."

When in doubt tell the truth.

—*Following the Equator*, 1897, vol. 1 ch. 2

If you tell the truth you don't have to remember anything.

—Notebook, 1894

Why *shouldn't* truth be stranger than fiction? Fiction, after all, has to stick to possibilities.

—*Following the Equator*, 1897, vol. 1, ch. 15

My own luck has been curious all my literary life; I never could tell a lie that anyone would doubt, nor a truth that anybody would believe.

—*Following the Equator*, 1897, vol. 2, ch. 26

It was ever thus, all through my life: whenever I have diverged from custom and principle and uttered a truth, the rule has been that the hearer hadn't strength of mind to believe it.

—Neider, *Autobiography*, 1959, ch. 26

Never tell the truth to people who are not worthy of it.

—Notebook, 1902

An injurious truth has no merit over an injurious lie. Neither should ever be uttered.

—"On the Decay of the Art of Lying," speech, 1881

There have been innumerable Temporary Seekers after the Truth—have you ever heard of a permanent one?

—"What Is Man?" essay, 1906

Truth is the most valuable thing we have. Let us economize it.

—*Following the Equator*, 1897, vol. 1, ch. 7

TWAIN, MARK

Mark Twain once visited a friend named Anson Burlingame in Hawaii. Burlingame suggested they go for a walk, and when Twain hesitated, Burlingame declared, "But there is a scriptural command for you to go."

"If you can quote one, I'll obey," said Mark Twain.

Burlingame offered this biblical injunction: "If any man require thee to walk a mile, go with him twain."

Twain went with him.

I was a fresh, new journalist, and needed a *nom de guerre;* so I confiscated the ancient mariner's discarded one, "Mark Twain," and have done my best to make it remain what it was in his hands—a sign and symbol and warrant that whatever is found in its company may be gambled on as being the petrified truth.

—*Life on the Mississippi*, 1883, ch. 50

TWIN

Mark Twain used to tell the sad story of his twin brother, Bill. When he and his twin brother were born, said Twain, the two looked so much alike that no one, not even their mother, could tell them apart. One day while a nurse was bathing the twin babies, one of them slipped into the depths of the tub and was drowned. No one could tell which twin was dead and which wasn't. "Therein was the tragedy," said Mark Twain. "Most people thought I was the one that lived, but I wasn't. *I was the one that drowned.*"

TYPEWRITER

Always fascinated by new inventions, Mark Twain prided himself on being among the first to take advantage of new technology.

Although he failed to invest in the telephone when he had the opportunity, he was one of the very first to own a telephone. And he was also one of the first writers to employ the typewriter.

"I have claimed that I was the first person in the world that ever had a telephone in his house for practical purposes; I will now claim—until dispossessed—that I was the first person in the world to *apply the typewriter to literature.*"

This was in 1874. "The early machine was full of caprices, full of defects—devilish ones. It had as many immoralities as the machine of today has virtues," he recalled. Whenever he typed on that typewriter the atmosphere swelled with the sounds of his swearing. "After a year or two I found that it was degrading my character, so I thought I would give it to Howells." Twain generously bestowed the typewriter, which he called a "little joker," on his friend and fellow novelist, William Dean Howells. "He took it home to Boston, and my morals began to improve, but his have never recovered."

UNCONSCIOUS HUMOR

In the Gospel According to Mark Twain, there are two types of humor: conscious and unconscious. Conscious humor is a deliberate attempt to be funny, for example, by telling a joke. Unconscious humor is unintentional, yet often contains more truth. Twain cited the example of "the Sunday school boy who defined a lie as 'An abomination before the Lord and an ever present help in time of trouble.' That may have been unconscious humor, but it looked more like hard, cold experience and knowledge of facts."

UNTRUTHS

In God We Trust. I don't believe it would sound any better if it were true.

—Notebook, 1904

Truth is mighty and will prevail. There is nothing the matter with this, except that it ain't so.

—Notebook, 1898

VALET

One day as Mark Twain was checking into the Waldorf-Astoria Hotel in New York, he noticed that the man who signed the register before him had written, with a rather affected flourish, "William Butler Conroy, and Valet."

Mark Twain signed in, "Samuel Clemens and valise."

VANITY

There are no grades of vanity, there are only grades of ability in concealing it.

—Notebook, 1898

Forty years ago I was not so good-looking. A looking glass then lasted me three months. Now I can wear it out in two days.

—Paine, *Autobiography*, 1924, vol. 2, p. 202

VICE

One day a derelict approached Mark Twain on the street in Hartford and asked him for a handout. Mark Twain sympathized with the unfortunate fellow and offered to buy him a drink.

The tramp said he didn't drink.

"How about a cigar?" suggested Mark Twain.

"Sir, I'm hungry," said the tramp, "but I don't smoke."

"How would you like me to place a couple of dollars for you tomorrow on a sure-winner horse?" Mark Twain proposed.

"Sir, I may not be the most righteous man, but I never gamble," said the beggar, somewhat haughtily. "Please, can't you spare a quarter for something to eat?"

"I'll stake you to a whole dinner if you let me introduce you to Mrs. Clemens," said Mark Twain. "I want to show her what becomes of a man who doesn't smoke, drink, or gamble."

I haven't a particle of confidence in a man who has no redeeming petty vices whatever.

—Paine, *Mark Twain: A Biography*,
1912, vol. 3, Appendix E

William Davidson . . . had not a single vice, unless you call it a vice in a Scot to love Scotch.

—"General Miles and the Dog,"
speech, 1907

VIOLENCE

Mark Twain had a violent temper, but his sense of humor saved him from the gallows, more than likely, and he believed that *humor*, in the same way, could save the human race from self-destruction. As a young man, Twain had been tempted to violence many times, and he once had to leave Nevada to avoid prosecution for violating an anti-dueling statute. But as the wise guy matured into the wise man, he gradually learned the blessed tolerance that makes peace. "If a man should challenge me now," he said benignly in his old age, "I would go to that man and take him kindly and forgivingly by the hand and lead him to a quiet retired spot and *kill* him."

VIRTUE

Be virtuous and you will be eccentric.

—"Mental Photographs," *A Curious Dream*, 1872

Virtue has never been as respectable as money.

—*Innocents Abroad*, 1869, ch. 55

The weakest of all weak things is a virtue that has not been tested in the fire.

—Henderson, *Mark Twain*, 1912, p. 192

A crime persevered in a thousand centuries ceases to be a crime, and becomes a virtue.

—*Following the Equator*, 1897, vol. 2, ch. 27

WALKING

The true charm of pedestrianism does not lie in the walking, or in the scenery, but in the talking.

—*A Tramp Abroad*, 1880, vol. 1, ch. 23

WAR

A wanton waste of projectiles.

—"The Art of War," speech, 1881

There has never been a just one, never an honorable one—on the part of the instigator of the war.

—"The Mysterious Stranger," story, 1916, ch. 9

I notice that God is on both sides in this war; thus history repeats itself. But I am the only person who has noticed this; everybody here thinks He is playing the game for this side, and for this side only.

—Letter to William Dean Howells,
January 26, 1900

By the etiquette of war, it is permitted to none below the rank of newspaper correspondent to dictate to the general in the field.

—"The Art of War," speech, 1881

The Emperor sent his troops to the field with immense enthusiasm. He will lead them in person when they return.

—"European War," *The Curious Republic
of Gondour,* 1919

Before I had a chance in another war, the desire to kill people to whom I had not been introduced had passed away.

—Neider, *Autobiography,* 1959, ch. 15

To be a patriot, one had to say, and keep on saying, "Our Country, right or wrong," and urge on the little war. Have you not perceived that that phrase is an insult to the nation?

—"Glances at History," written 1906,
published 1962

Statesmen will invent cheap lies, putting blame upon the nation that is attacked, and every man will be glad of those conscience-soothing falsities, and will diligently study them, and refuse to examine any refutations of them; and thus he will by and by convince himself that the war *is* just, and will thank God for the better sleep he enjoys after this process of grotesque self-deception.

—"Chronicle of Young Satan," *A Pen
Warmed-Up in Hell,* 1972

An inglorious peace is better than a dishonorable war.

—"Glances at History," written 1906,
published 1962

"The War Prayer" was perhaps Mark Twain's most prophetic
piece of writing. He was advised by his family not to publish "The
War Prayer," which he dictated in 1904, because it would be
regarded as sacrilege. But he resolved that it should be published
after his death, and so it was, in 1916. "I have told the truth in
that," he said with some resignation, "and only dead men can tell
the truth in this world."

"The War Prayer" is a story that takes place on a Sunday in
church at a time when the nation is preparing for a war. The
preacher has just finished praying that God will guide the nation's
young soldiers safely to victory, when a mysterious stranger enters the church and declares, "I come from the Throne—bearing
a message from Almighty God! . . . If you would beseech a blessing
upon yourself, beware! lest without intent you invoke a curse
upon a neighbor at the same time. . . . When you have prayed for
victory you have prayed for many unmentioned results which
follow victory. . . . For it is like unto many of the prayers of men,
in that it asks for more than he who utters it is aware of—except
he pause and think."

The stranger then reveals why he has come. "Upon the listening spirit of God the Father also fell the unspoken part of the
prayer. He commandeth me to put it into words. Listen!"

O Lord our God, help us to tear their soldiers to bloody
shreds with our shells; help us to cover their smiling fields
with the pale forms of their patriot dead: help us to drown
the thunder of the guns with the shrieks of their wounded,
writhing in pain; help us to lay waste their humble homes
with a hurricane of fire; help us to wring the hearts of their
unoffending widows with unavailing grief; help us to turn
them out roofless with their little children to wander un-
friended the wastes of their desolated land in rags and hun-
ger and thirst, sports of the sun flames of summer and the icy
winds of winter, broken in spirit, worn with travail, implor-
ing Thee for the refuge of the grave and denied it— For our
sakes who adore Thee, Lord, blast their hopes, blight their
lives, protract their bitter pilgrimage, make heavy their steps,
water their way with tears, stain the white snow with the
blood of their wounded feet! We ask it in the spirit of love,

of him who is the Source of Love, and who is the ever-faithful refuge and friend of all who are sore beset and seek His aid with humble and contrite hearts. Amen.

WASHINGTON, D.C.

There is something good and motherly about Washington, the grand old benevolent National Asylum for the Helpless.

—*The Gilded Age,* 1873, ch. 24

That building is the Capitol . . . by the original estimates it was to cost $12,000,000 . . . the government did come within $27,200,-000 of building it for that sum.

—*The Gilded Age,* 1873, ch. 24

WASHINGTON, GEORGE

He was ignorant of the commonest accomplishments of youth. He could not even lie.

—Walker, *The Washoe Giant in San Francisco,* 1938, p. 107

WATERMELON

The true Southern watermelon is a boon apart, and not to be mentioned with the commoner things. It is chief of this world's luxuries, king by the grace of God over all the fruits of the earth. When one has tasted it, he knows what the angels eat. It was not a Southern watermelon that Eve took; we know it because she repented.

—*Pudd'nhead Wilson,* 1894, ch. 14

WEATHER

"Everybody talks about the weather but nobody does anything about it." This famous quip of Mark Twain's reflected his exasperation not only at man's inability to improve the weather but also at man's inability to come up with a more interesting topic of conversation.

One fine spring day, Mark Twain was hailed by every passing acquaintance with some remark upon the weather. Most of these remarks followed a similar pattern, which soon grew tedious in its sameness. Finally, he arrived at his destination, only to be greeted with, "Nice day, Mr. Twain."

Twain sighed and replied, "Yes, I've heard it highly spoken of."

WEATHER IN NOVELS

"Weather is a literary specialty, and no untrained hand can turn out a good article of it," Mark Twain wrote in the preface to his 1892 novel, *The American Claimant.* He recognized the necessity of including some weather in the novel. "Of course weather is necessary to a narrative of human experience. That is conceded. But it ought to be put where it will not be in the way; where it will not interrupt the flow of the narrative."

Mark Twain complained that many readers were impeded by bad weather. "Many a reader who wanted to read a tale through was not able to do it because of delays on account of the weather." He concluded: "Persistent intrusions of the weather are bad for both reader and author."

For this reason, Mark Twain left weather out of *The American Claimant,* and put it in an appendix in the back of the book, where it would be "out of the way." This appendix contains selected descriptions of weather for the reader to use as needed. "The reader is requested to turn over and help himself from time to time as he goes along."

WEDDING INVITATIONS

Who has never received an unwanted wedding invitation? Certainly not Mark Twain. He once replied to a soon-to-be-bride, "I will if you'll come to my funeral."

Unfortunately, this did not discourage her as much as he had hoped. She agreed to the terms, enthusiastically. Twain added: "And now she's quite eager for it to happen."

WELCOME

A most moving and pulse-stirring honor—the heartfelt grip of the hand, and the welcome that does not descend from the pale, gray matter of the brain but rushes up with the red blood of the heart.

—"The Begum of Bengal," speech
1907

WINTER

It is a time when one's spirit is subdued and sad, one knows not why; when the past seems a storm-swept desolation, life a vanity and a burden, and the future but a way to death.

—*The Gilded Age,* 1873, ch. 60
(on a bleak winter day)

WIT

Wit is the sudden marriage of ideas which, before their union, were not perceived to have any relation.

—Notebook, 1885

Wit, by itself, is of little account. It becomes of moment only when grounded on wisdom.

—Fisher, *Abroad with Mark Twain,*
1922, p. 218

WIVES

Mark Twain was opposed to polygamy in principle when he first arrived in Salt Lake City, where the Mormon leader Brigham Young was situated with his sixty wives. But when Twain first caught a glimpse of Brigham Young's homely wives, he changed his mind.

"I was touched. My heart was wiser than my head. It warmed toward these poor, ungainly, and pathetically 'homely' creatures, and as I turned to hide the generous moisture in my eyes, I said, 'No—the man that marries one of them has done an act of Christian charity which entitles him to the kindly applause of mankind, not their harsh censure—and the man that marries sixty of them

246

has done a deed of open-handed generosity so sublime that the nations should stand uncovered in his presence and worship in silence."

WOMAN

"Human intellect cannot estimate what we owe to woman," declared Mark Twain in an 1868 toast to the fair sex. "She gives us good advice, and plenty of it, she soothes our aching brows, she bears our children—ours as a general thing."

He continued his tribute: "In whatever position you place a woman she is an ornament to society and a treasure to the world. As a sweetheart she has few equals and no superiors. As a cousin she is convenient. As a wealthy grandmother with an incurable distemper she is precious."

Paying homage to some of the great women of history, Twain proclaimed: "Look at Cleopatra! Look at Desdemona! Look at Florence Nightingale! Look at Joan of Arc! Look at Lucretia Borgia! Well, suppose we let Lucretia slide."

Mark Twain concluded on a sentimental note. "What, sir, would the people of the earth be without woman? They would be scarce, sir, almighty scarce."

There is only one good sex. The female one.

—Attributed

One frequently only finds out how really beautiful a beautiful woman is after considerable acquaintance with her.

—*Innocents Abroad,* 1869, ch. 54

Men and women—even man and wife are foreigners. Each has reserves that the other cannot enter into, nor understand.

—Notebook, 1904

No civilization can be perfect until exact equality between man and woman is included.

—Notebook, 1895

It takes much to convince the average man of anything; and perhaps nothing can ever make him realize he is the average woman's inferior—yet in several important details the evidence seems to show that that is what he is.

—Following the Equator, 1897, vol. 1, ch. 32

Man has ruled the human race from the beginning—but he should remember that up to the middle of the present century it was a dull world, and ignorant and stupid; but it is not such a dull world now, and is growing less and less dull all the time. This is woman's opportunity—she has had none before.

—Following the Equator, 1897, vol. 1, ch. 32

WORDS

At an Associated Press banquet in New York in 1906, Mark Twain told how he was once employed by a ruthless magazine editor who paid him only seven cents a word, regardless of the length of the words.

One day, Twain was given the assignment to write ten pages on this revolting text: "Considerations concerning the alleged subterranean holophotal extemporaneousness of the conchyliaceous superimbrication of the ornithorhyncus."

Stalking up to the editor's desk, Mark Twain demanded to be hired by the year. The editor refused. Twain pleaded, "You ought to at least allow me overtime on that word 'extemporaneousness.'"

"Again he coldly refused," Twain recounted with a shudder. "I seldom say a harsh word to anyone, but I was not master of myself then, and I spoke right out and called him an anisodactylous plesiosaurian conchyliaceous ornithorhyncus, and rotten to the heart with holophotal subterranean extemporaneousness. God forgive me for that wanton crime; he lived only two hours."

WORK

"I love work," confessed Mark Twain. "Why, sir, when I have a piece of work to perform, I go away to myself, sit down in the shade, and muse over the coming enjoyment. Sometimes I muse too long."

Perhaps the best-known of all of Mark Twain's stories is the story of Tom Sawyer whitewashing the fence, which shows that the difference between work and play is a matter of attitude.

At first, Tom Sawyer is disconsolate because he is forced to work on a Saturday while his friends are at liberty to play: "Tom appeared on the sidewalk with a bucket of whitewash and a long-handled brush. He surveyed the fence, and all gladness left him and a deep melancholy settled down upon his spirit. Thirty yards of board fence nine feet high. Life to him seemed hollow, and existence but a burden."

When his friend Ben Rogers stops by to taunt him for working, Tom Sawyer pretends to be enjoying himself immensely.

"Hello, old chap, you got to work, hey?"
"What do you call work?"
"Why, ain't *that* work?"
"Well, maybe it is and maybe it ain't. All I know is, it suits Tom Sawyer. . . . Does a boy get to whitewash a fence every day?"

That put the thing in a new light. Before long, Ben Rogers is begging Tom Sawyer to let *him* do some whitewashing.

Lest we should fail to learn the lesson, Mark Twain tells us the moral of the tale, after Tom Sawyer has inveigled his friends into completing the whitewashing for him. "He had discovered a great law of human action, without knowing it—namely that in order to make a man or a boy covet a thing, it is only necessary to make the thing difficult to attain. If he had been a great and wise philosopher, like the writer of this book, he would now have comprehended that Work consists of whatever a body is *obliged* to do and that Play consists of whatever a body is not obliged to do."

When we talk about the great workers of the world we really mean the great players of the world.

—"A Humorist's Confession," *New York Times*, 1905

What work I have done I have done because it has been play. If it had been work I shouldn't have done it.

—"A Humorist's Confession," New York Times, 1905

Intellectual "work" is misnamed; it is a pleasure, a dissipation, and is its own highest reward.

—A Connecticut Yankee, 1889, ch. 28

The law of work does seem utterly unfair—but there it is: the higher the pay in enjoyment the worker gets out of it, the higher shall be his pay in cash, also.

—A Connecticut Yankee, 1889, ch. 28

WORRY

As soon as one is at rest, in this world, off he goes on something else to worry about.

—A Connecticut Yankee, 1889, ch. 5

"Don't you worry, and don't you hurry." I know that phrase by heart, and if all the other music should perish out of the world it would still sing to me.

—"Home Conditions," speech, 1900

WRITERS

When an honest writer discovers an imposition it is his simple duty to strip it bare and hurl it down from its place of honor, no matter who suffers by it; any other course would render him unworthy of the public confidence.

—A Tramp Abroad, 1880, vol. 1, ch. 26

WRITING

Mark Twain was a professional writer, but he was never the kind of professional writer who wrote what he was told to write. He always insisted on writing exactly what he pleased. "If a man comes to me and says, 'Mr. Clemens, I want you to write me a story,' I'll write it for him; but if he undertakes to tell me what to write I'll say, 'Go hire a typewriter.'"

It is difficult to summarize Mark Twain's thoughts on the craft of writing, for he never produced a literary manifesto, and his own writing employed a wide variety of styles. He is best known as a humorist, and as a humorist he is unsurpassed. But his success as a humorist has, if anything, delayed his recognition as one of the world's greatest masters of literature. Certainly he was a great innovator in the use of vernacular, colloquialism and dialect. As he warned the reader in the preface of *Huckleberry Finn,* "In this book a number of dialects are used. . . . I make this explanation for the reason that without it many readers would suppose that all these characters were trying to talk alike and not succeeding."

Perhaps Mark Twain's greatest contribution as a writer was in freeing the American language from the formal straitjacket of literary prose. As H. L. Mencken noted in his book *The American Language,* "He was the first American author of world rank to write a genuinely colloquial and native American."

Though he created the illusion of spontaneous speech, Mark Twain was nevertheless a careful craftsman. He loathed long, literary descriptions. "As to the Adjective: when in doubt, strike it out." He tried to make every word count. "With a hundred words to do it with, the literary artisan could catch that airy thought and tie it down and reduce it to a . . . cabbage, but the artist does it with twenty, and the result is a flower."

He warned against excessive stage directions in fiction. "Some authors overdo the stage directions," he wrote in 1906, "they elaborate them quite beyond necessity; they spend so much time and take up so much room in telling us how a person said a thing and how he looked and acted when he said it that we get tired and vexed and wish he hadn't said it at all."

But some writers had too few stage directions in stock. "Writers of this school go in rags, in the matter of stage directions; the majority of them have nothing in stock but a cigar, a laugh, a blush, and a bursting into tears."

For aspiring writers, Mark Twain offered this advice: "Write without pay until somebody offers pay. If nobody offers within three years, the candidate may look upon this circumstance with the most implicit confidence as the sign that sawing wood is what he was intended for."

The difference between the right word and the almost right word is the difference between lightning and the lightning bug.

—Letter dated October 15, 1888

There is only one right form for a story and if you fail to find that form the story will not tell itself.

—Neider, *Autobiography,* 1959, ch. 53

I conceive that the right way to write a story for boys is to write so that it will not only interest boys but strongly interest any man who has ever been a boy. That immensely enlarges the audience.

—Letter to Fred Hall, August 10, 1892

I confine myself to life with which I am familiar when pretending to portray life.

—Paine, *Mark Twain's Letters,* 1917,
vol. 2, p. 541

The time to begin writing an article is when you have finished it to your satisfaction. By that time you begin to clearly and logically perceive what it is that you really want to say.

—Notebook, 1902

A successful book is not made of what is in it, but what is left out of it.

—Letter to William Dean Howells,
February 23, 1897

I never write *metropolis* for seven cents because I can get the same price for *city.* I never write *policeman* because I can get the same money for *cop.*

—"Simplified Spelling," speech, 1906

How often I do use three words where one would answer—a thing I am always trying to guard against.

—Letter to William Dean Howells,
1875

I made the great discovery that when the tank runs dry you've only to leave it alone and it will fill up again in time, while you are asleep—also while you are at work on other things and are quite unaware that this unconscious and profitable cerebration is going on.

—Neider, *Autobiography*, 1959, ch. 53

WRITING, RULES OF

There are nineteen rules governing literary art in the domain of romantic fiction—some say twenty-two. In *Deerslayer*, Cooper violated eighteen of them. These eighteen require:

1. That a tale shall accomplish something and arrive somewhere.

2. That the episodes of a tale shall be necessary parts of the tale and shall help to develop it.

3. That the personages in a tale shall be alive, except in the case of corpses, and that always the reader shall be able to tell the corpses from the others.

4. That the personages in a tale, both dead and alive, shall exhibit a sufficient excuse for being there.

5. That when the personages of a tale deal in conversation, the talk shall sound like human talk, and be talk such as human beings would be likely to talk in the given circumstances, and have a discoverable meaning, also a discoverable purpose and a show of relevancy, and remain in the neighborhood of the subject at hand, and be interesting to the reader, and help out the tale, and stop when the people cannot think of anything more to say.

6. That when the author describes the character of a personage in his tale, the conduct and conversation of that personage shall justify said description.

7. That when a person talks like an illustrated, gilt-edged, tree-calf, hand-tooled, seven-dollar Friendship's Offering in the beginning of a paragraph, he shall not talk like a Negro minstrel in the end of it.

8. That crass stupidities shall not be played upon the reader as "the craft of the woodsman, the delicate art of the forest," by either the author or the people in the tale.

9. That the personages in the tale shall confine themselves to possibilities and let miracles alone; or, if they venture a miracle, the author must so plausibly set it forth as to make it look possible and reasonable.

10. That the author shall make the reader feel a deep interest in the personages of his tale and in their fate, and that he shall make the reader love the good people in the tale and hate the bad ones.

11. That the characters in the tale shall be so clearly defined that the reader can tell beforehand what each will do in a given emergency.

12. The author shall *say* what he is proposing to say, not merely come near it.

13. Use the right word, not its second cousin.

14. Eschew surplusage.

15. Not omit necessary details.

16. Avoid slovenliness of form.

17. Use good grammar.

18. Employ a simple and straightforward style.

—"Fenimore Cooper's Literary
Offenses," essay, 1895

YOUTH

"When I was a boy of fourteen, my father was so ignorant I could hardly stand to have the old man around. But when I got to be twenty-one, I was astonished at how much he had learned in seven years."

This famous remark of Mark Twain's cannot be taken too literally, for his own father died when he was eleven. His father's death brought to an abrupt end the childhood that was immortalized in that hymn to lost childhood called *The Adventures of Tom Sawyer*. After his father's death, young Samuel Clemens was forced to go to work in the adult world, first as a printer's apprentice, later as a river pilot, a miner and a journalist. Ultimately he found his true calling as Mark Twain, America's greatest storyteller. But he never lost his youth, that ineffable quality which found expression in his playfulness and his humor.

It was no coincidence that his wife always called him Youth. In his autobiography, he offered a partial explanation: "Youth . . . was my wife's pet name for me. It was gently satirical and also affectionate. I had certain mental and material peculiarities and customs proper to a person much younger than I."

Rudyard Kipling spotted this quality in Mark Twain immediately on meeting him for the first time, in Elmira, New York, in the summer of 1889. He described it as well as anyone ever has: "The thing that first struck me was that he was an elderly man; yet, after a minute's thought, I perceived that it was otherwise, and in five minutes, the eyes looking at me, I saw that the gray hair was an accident of the most trivial. He was quite young."

I am just as young now as I was 40 years ago.

> —*Baltimore News,* 1909

There is no sadder sight than a young pessimist.

> —Notebook, 1902

It is a pity that we cannot escape from life when we are young.

> —Neider, *Autobiography,* 1959, ch. 25

The tragedies of maturer life cannot surpass the first tragedies of youth.

> —Clara Clemens, *My Husband,*
> *Gabrilowitsch,* 1938, p. 8

The Young can sink into abysses of despondency—but the hopes of the young are quick to rise again.

> —*Joan of Arc,* 1896, bk. 3, ch. 23

The elastic heart of youth cannot be compressed into one constrained shape long at a time.

> —*Tom Sawyer,* 1876, ch. 8

It is good to obey all the rules when you're young, so you'll have the strength to break them when you're old.

—*Advance Magazine,* February 1940

May you always keep your youth.

—"Simplified Spelling," speech, 1906
(saluting audience at conclusion of
speech)

AFTERWORD
by Alex Ayres

WHAT MARK TWAIN MIGHT SAY TODAY

On America

We all love our country. It's our countrymen we have trouble with.

On Americans

Americans are a deeply religious people. You can tell by the way they drive.

On Christianity

Christianity is a great idea that's never been tried.

On Communism

My criticism of communism is that under communism it isn't allowed.

On Divorce

In love, you pay as you leave.

On Extraterrestrial Intelligence

Intelligent life may exist on many planets in the universe—including the earth. But so far, we just don't have enough evidence.

On Goodness

A good person is somebody who does good, but usually not very well.

On History

History doesn't repeat itself—it stutters.

On Knowledge

What you don't know can't hurt you—unless you're still alive.

On Life

It's not what you've done that matters—it's what you haven't done.

On Life After Death

Yes, there is life after death. But please don't tell the IRS.

On Lunch

We used to say, "Good riddance!" Now we say, "Let's have lunch sometime!"

On the National Debt

What are we going to do when the national debt reaches infinity? Bring back Gerald Ford and ask him to pardon it?

On Old Age

You know you are getting old when you tell your doctor you are *not* dead and he argues with you.

On Patriotism

During the Los Angeles Olympics, we Americans learned the true meaning of *patriotism*—it's that vague feeling of resentment you get when somebody from another country comes in first.

On Peace

Love your enemy—it will scare the hell out of him.

On Prices

You don't always get what you pay for. But you always pay for what you get.

On Responsibility

Have you ever noticed that no matter what goes wrong, it's not really your fault?

On Self-Love

Self-love was the major social movement of the 1970s. Falling in love with yourself is easy—the hard part is breaking up.

On Terrorism

Terrorists are high-minded idealists who assassinate innocent men, women and children for a good cause.

On the Unborn

Sometimes the kindest thing we can do for the unborn is to let them stay that way.

On the Vietnam War

The painful lesson of the Vietnam War is clear. We should never fight a war unless we have been attacked and our country is in danger—or unless we are sure we can win.

On Waiting

People spend too much time waiting in lines. There are two things you should never have to wait in line to do: one is to go to the bathroom; the other is to make love.

On Women

Statistics show that women live longer than men; but that's hardly surprising. A woman always takes longer to get ready—for anything.

BIBLIOGRAPHY

American Academy of Arts and Letters. "In Memory of Samuel Lang-
horne Clemens." 1922.

Anderson, F., ed. *A Pen Warmed-Up in Hell: Mark Twain in Protest.* Harper
& Row, 1972.

Bok, E. *The Americanization of Edward Bok.* Scribner's, 1912.

Brown, R. B., ed. *Mark Twain's Quarrel with Heaven.* College & University
Press, 1970.

Casseres, B. *When Huck Finn Went Highbrow.* Thomas F. Madigan, 1934.

Clemens, C. *My Father, Mark Twain.* Harper, 1931.

Clemens, C. *My Husband, Gabrilowitsch.* Harper, 1938

Clemens, S. I. *The Curious Republic of Gondour.* Boni & Liveright, 1919.

Clemens, W. *Mark Twain, His Life and Work.* F. Tennyson Needly, 1894.

DeVoto, B., ed. *Letters from the Earth.* Harper & Row, 1962.

DeVoto, B., ed. *Mark Twain in Eruption.* Harper, 1940.

Fatout, P. *Mark Twain in Virginia City.* Indiana University Press, 1964.

Fatout, P. *Mark Twain on the Lecture Circuit.* Indiana University Press, 1960.

Fatout, P., ed. *Mark Twain Speaking.* University of Iowa Press, 1976.

Ficklen, A., ed. *The Hidden Mark Twain: A Collection of Little Known Mark
Twain.* Crown, 1984.

Fisher, E. *Abroad with Mark Twain and Eugene Field.* Nicholas L. Brown, 1922.

Freud, S. *Jokes and Their Relation to the Unconscious.* Trans. by J. Strachey. W.
W. Norton, 1963.

Galaxy Magazine. "Memoranda." May, August, December, 1870.

Hannibal Courier-Post. Centennial Edition of Mark Twain's Birth, March 6,
1935.

Harper's Magazine. "Unpublished Chapters from the Autobiography of
Mark Twain." August 1922.

Harte, B., and Twain, M. *Sketches of the Sixties.* John Howell, 1926.

Henderson, A. *Mark Twain.* Stokes, 1912.

Holbrook, H. *Mark Twain Tonight: An Actor's Portrait.* Washburn, 1959.

Howells, W. D. *My Mark Twain.* Harper, 1910.

Johnson, M. *A Bibliography of Mark Twain.* Harper, 1935.

Johnson, M. *More Maxims of Mark.* Privately printed, 1927.

Johnson, R. U. *Remembered Yesterdays.* Little, Brown, 1923.

Kaplan, Justin. *Mr. Clemens and Mark Twain.* Simon & Schuster, 1966.

Lawton, M. *A Lifetime with Mark Twain.* Harcourt, Brace, 1925.

Lorch, F. "Mark Twain in Iowa." *Iowa Journal of History and Politics.* July and October, 1929.

MacLaren, G. *Morally We Roll Along.* Little, Brown, 1938.

Macy, J. *Mark Twain.* Doubleday, 1913.

Masson, T. L. *Best Stories in the World.* Doubleday, 1913.

Neider, C., ed. *The Autobiography of Mark Twain.* Harper & Row, 1959.

Neider, C., ed. *The Complete Essays of Mark Twain.* Doubleday, 1963.

Neider, C., ed. *The Complete Short Stories of Mark Twain.* Doubleday, 1957.

Neider, C., ed. *Plymouth Rock and the Pilgrims and Other Salutary Platform Opinions.* Harper & Row, 1984.

Neider, C., ed. *The Selected Letters of Mark Twain.* Harper & Row, 1982.

North American Review. "Chapters from My Autobiography." November 1906, January, March, April, May, September, 1907.

Orcutt, W. E. *Celebrities Off Parade.* Willet, Clark, 1935.

Paine, A. B. *Mark Twain: A Biography.* Harper, 1912.

Paine, A. B. *Moments with Mark Twain.* Harper, 1920.

Paine, A. B., ed. *Mark Twain's Autobiography.* Harper, 1924.

Paine, A. B., ed. *Mark Twain's Letters.* Harper, 1917.

Paine, A. B., ed. *Mark Twain's Notebook.* Harper, 1935.

Paine, A. B., ed. *Mark Twain's Speeches.* Harper, 1910, 1923.

Phelps, W. L. *Autobiography with Letters.* Oxford University Press, 1939.

Pond, J. B. *The Eccentricities of Genius.* G. W. Dillingham, 1900.

Quick, D. "Mark Twain's Friendship Inspired Little Girl to Successful Career." *Advance Magazine.* February 1940.

Read, O. *Mark Twain and I.* Reilly, Lee, 1940.

Reader's Digest. May 1934, March 1937, September 1937, December 1944.

Teacher, L., ed. *The Unabridged Mark Twain.* Running Press, 1976.

Tucker, J. S., ed. *The Devil's Race-Track: Mark Twain's Great Dark Writings.* University of California Press, 1966.

Twain, M. *The Adventures of Huckleberry Finn.* Charles Webster & Co., 1884.

Twain, M. *The Adventures of Thomas Jefferson Snodgrass.* Covici, 1928.

Twain, M. *The Adventures of Tom Sawyer.* American Publishing Co., 1877.

Twain, M. *The American Claimant.* Webster & Co., 1892.

Twain, M. *Captain Stormfield's Visit to Heaven.* Harper, 1907.

Twain, M. *The Celebrated Jumping Frog of Calaveras County.* C. H. Webb, 1867.

Twain, M. *Christian Science.* Harper, 1907.

Twain, M. *A Connecticut Yankee in King Arthur's Court.* Webster & Co., 1889.

Twain, M. *The Double-Barrelled Detective Story.* Harper, 1902.

Twain, M. *Europe and Elsewhere.* Harper, 1923.

Twain, M. *Eve's Diary.* Harper, 1906.

Twain, M. *Extracts from Adam's Diary.* Harper, 1904.

Twain, M. *Following the Equator.* American Publishing Co., 1897.

Twain, M. *The Innocents Abroad.* American Publishing Co., 1869.

Twain, M. *Is Shakespeare Dead?* Harper, 1909.

Twain, M. *Letters from the Sandwich Islands.* Stanford University Press, 1938.

Twain, M. *Life on the Mississippi.* Osgood & Co., 1883.

Twain, M. *Mark Twain's Letters to Will Bowen.* University of Texas Press, 1941.

Twain, M. *The Mysterious Stranger.* Harper, 1916.

Twain, M. *Personal Recollections of Joan of Arc.* Harper, 1896.

Twain, M. *The Prince and the Pauper.* Osgood & Co., 1882.

Twain, M. *Roughing It.* American Publishing Co., 1872.

Twain, M. *"1601" or, Conversation at the Social Fireside As It Was in the Time of the Tudors.* Grabhorn Press, 1925.

Twain, M. *Sketches New and Old.* American Publishing Co., 1875.

Twain, M. *The Stolen White Elephant.* Osgood & Co., 1882.

Twain, M. *Tom Sawyer, Detective, and Other Stories.* Harper, 1896.

Twain, M. *Tom Sawyer Abroad.* Webster & Co., 1894.

Twain, M. *The Tragedy of Pudd'nhead Wilson.* American Publishing Co., 1894.

Twain, M. *A Tramp Abroad.* American Publishing Co., 1880.

Twain, M. *What Is Man?* Privately printed, 1906.

Twain, M. *What Is Man? and Other Essays.* Harper, 1917.

Twain, M. and Warner, C. D. *The Gilded Age.* American Publishing Co., 1873.

Wagenknecht, E. *Mark Twain, the Man and His Work.* Yale University Press, 1935.

Walker, F., ed. *The Washoe Giant in San Francisco.* George Fields, 1938.

Walker, F., and Dane, G. E., eds. *Mark Twain's Travels with Mr. Brown.* Knopf, 1940.

Wallace, E. *Mark Twain and the Happy Island.* A. C. McClurg, 1913.

Webster, S. C. *Mark Twain, Business Man.* Little, Brown, 1944.

Wecter, D., ed. *The Love Letters of Mark Twain.* Harper, 1949.

Wilson, F. *Francis Wilson's Life of Himself.* Houghton Mifflin, 1924.

Youth's Companion. "A Letter from Mark Twain." May 18, 1882.

Zali, P. *Mark Twain Laughing.* University of Tennessee Press, 1985.

PLUME TICKLES YOUR FUNNYBONE

PLUME 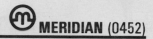 **MERIDIAN** (0452)

THE FLAMES OF DISSENT

☐ **KAFFIR BOY by Mark Mathabane.** Growing up in devastating poverty in South Africa, Mark Mathabane learned to measure his life in days, not years. This is the extraordinary memoir of life under apartheid where bloody gang wars and midnight police raids were the rites of passage of a young black boy coming of age   (264715—$9.95)

☐ **MAKEBA by Miriam Makeba with James Hall.** Mirial Makeba. A singer, a woman, an outspoken South African civil rights activist... This is the story of her remarkable life— a life that encompasses the splendor of international acclaim, bitter personal tragedy, political intrigue and violence, and the irrepressible power and triumph of a brilliant talent. "Absorbing...her memories are both fascinating reading and important documentation."—*The New York Times*   (262348—$9.95)

☐ **LET THE TRUMPET SOUND: THE LIFE OF MARTIN LUTHER KING, JR. by Stephen B. Oates.** Through this brilliant examination of the forces that shaped him—parental, cultural, spiritual, and intellectual—and of the force he became at a crucial moment in America's history, Oates shows us the real Martin Luther King, not an abstract symbol but a man a very human man and a very great one.   (256275—$10.95)

☐ **DEATH AT AN EARLY AGE by Jonathan Kozol.** In 1964, Jonathon Kozol entered the Boston Public School System to teach at one of its most crowded inner-city schools. This book is his own unsparing account of the year he spent here—the most shocking and powerful personal story ever told by a young teacher.   (262925—$8.95)

Prices slightly higher in Canada.

Buy them at your local bookstore or use this convenient
coupon for ordering.

NEW AMERICAN LIBRARY
P.O. Box 999, Bergenfield, New Jersey 07621

Please send me the books I have checked above. I am enclosing $ _____
(please add $1.50 to this order to cover postage and handling). Send check or
money order—no cash or C.O.D.'s. Prices and numbers are subject to change
without notice.

Name _____

Address_____

City _____ State _____ Zip Code _____
Allow 4-6 weeks for delivery.
This offer is subject to withdrawal without notice.

There's an epidemic with 27 million victims. And no visible symptoms.

It's an epidemic of people who can't read.

Believe it or not, 27 million Americans are functionally illiterate, about one adult in five.

The solution to this problem is you... when you join the fight against illiteracy. So call the Coalition for Literacy at toll-free **1-800-228-8813** and volunteer.

Volunteer Against Illiteracy. The only degree you need is a degree of caring.